OFFICIAL SQA PAST PAPERS WITH ANSWERS

STANDARD GRADE | GENERAL | CREDIT

CRAFT & DESIGN
2006-2010

BrightRED PUBLISHING

© Scottish Qualifications Authority

All rights reserved. Copying prohibited. No part of this publication may be reproduced, stored in a retrieval system, or transmitted in any form or by any means, electronic, mechanical, photocopying, recording or otherwise.

First exam published in 2006.
Published by Bright Red Publishing Ltd, 6 Stafford Street, Edinburgh EH3 7AU
tel: 0131 220 5804 fax: 0131 220 6710 info@brightredpublishing.co.uk www.brightredpublishing.co.uk

ISBN 978-1-84948-085-7

A CIP Catalogue record for this book is available from the British Library.

Bright Red Publishing is grateful to the copyright holders, as credited on the final page of the book, for permission to use their material.
Every effort has been made to trace the copyright holders and to obtain their permission for the use of copyright material.
Bright Red Publishing will be happy to receive information allowing us to rectify any error or omission in future editions.

STANDARD GRADE | GENERAL

2006

[BLANK PAGE]

G

FOR OFFICIAL USE

Total

0600/402

NATIONAL	MONDAY, 8 MAY	CRAFT AND DESIGN
QUALIFICATIONS	G/C 1.35 PM – 2.35 PM	STANDARD GRADE
2006	F/G 2.35 PM – 3.35 PM	General Level

Fill in these boxes and read what is printed below.

Full name of centre

Town

Forename(s)

Surname

Date of birth
Day Month Year

Scottish candidate number

Number of seat

1 Answer all the questions.

2 Read every question carefully before you answer.

3 Write your answers in the spaces provided.

4 Do **not** write in the margins.

5 All dimensions are given in millimetres.

6 Before leaving the examination room you must give this book to the invigilator. If you do not, you may lose all the marks for this paper.

SCOTTISH
QUALIFICATIONS
AUTHORITY

©

ATTEMPT ALL QUESTIONS

1. An acrylic toothbrush holder is shown below.

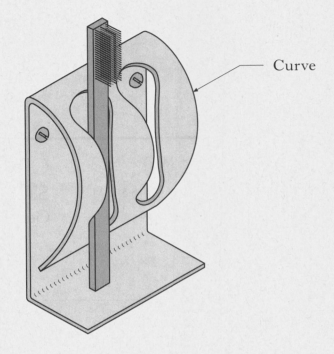

Curve

(a) State **three** reasons why acrylic is a suitable material for the holder.

Reason 1 _____

Reason 2 _____

Reason 3 _____

(b) State **two** factors that would affect the overall size of the holder.

Factor 1 _____

Factor 2 _____

(c) List **four** stages in finishing the edges of the acrylic.

Stage 1 _____

Stage 2 _____

Stage 3 _____

Stage 4 _____

1. **(continued)**

(*d*) Two holes were drilled in the back of the holder to allow it to be fixed to a wall.

State the name of the tool used to hold the acrylic while drilling.

_____

1
0

(*e*) State the name of the equipment used to heat the acrylic prior to bending the **curve**.

_____

_____

1
0

(*f*) The screw below was supplied with the holder for fixing it to a wall.

(i) State the type of head on this screw.

_____

1
0

(ii) The holder is to be used in a damp atmosphere. State why steel screws are unsuitable in this situation.

_____

1
0

(iii) State a suitable material for the screws.

_____

1
0

[Turn over

2. A fruit bowl manufactured from aluminium is shown below.

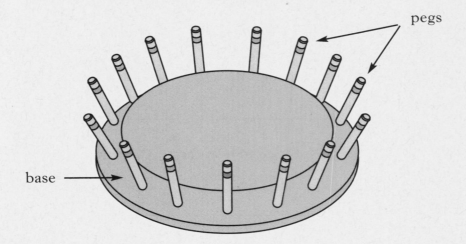

pegs

base

(a) (i) A peg manufactured using a metal lathe is shown below. On the diagram, indicate where the following processes have been carried out. Process (A) has been done for you.

3
2
1
0

(A)

(A) Knurling
(B) Parallel turning
(C) Chamfering
(D) Facing

(ii) State the reason for carrying out the process (C).

1
0

_____

(iii)

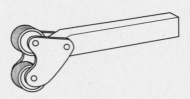

The tool shown above was used during the manufacture of the peg.

State which process was carried out using this tool.

1
0

_____

2.   **(continued)**

(*b*)   The end of the peg shown is to be threaded.

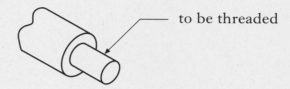

to be threaded

(i)   The tool used to cut the thread is shown.

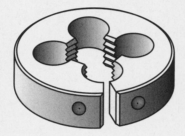

State the name of this tool.

_____

1
0

(ii)   State **one** method of ensuring a high quality thread is cut.

_____

1
0

(*c*)   The base was cast in aluminium.

Some terms relating to the casting process are given below.

Runner   Riser   Crucible   Pattern   Vent hole

Use the above terms to complete the following sentences.

(i)   A _____ is a wooden copy of the shape to be cast.

1
0

(ii)   A _____ holds the molten aluminium during heating.

1
0

(iii)   The _____ is where the aluminium is poured into the mould.

1
0

[Turn over

DO NO
WRITE
THIS
MARGI

3. A bench made from solid timber is shown below.

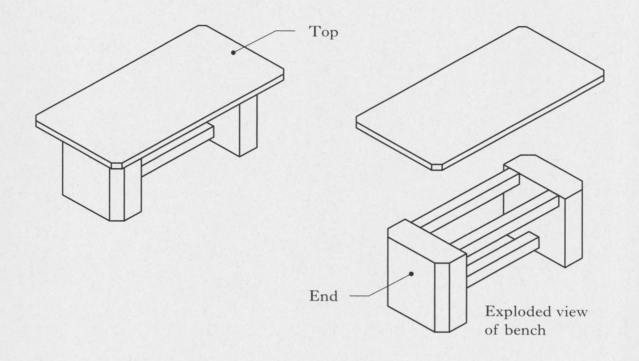

Top

End

Exploded view
of bench

(a) State **two** human dimensions which would be important in the design of the bench.

Dimension 1 _____

Dimension 2 _____

1
0
1
0

(b) The joint shown was used in the manufacture of the bench.

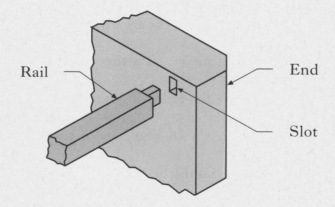

Rail

End

Slot

(i) State the name of this joint. _____

1
0

3. (b) (continued)

   (ii) Name the hand tool which could be used to:

      (A) mark lines across the rail _____ .

      (B) mark two parallel lines along the rail _____ .

      (C) saw the joint on the rail _____ .

      (D) cut the slot in the end_____ .

   (c) This tool was used during the manufacture of the table.

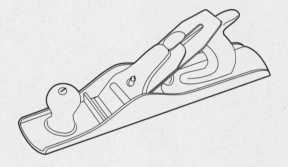

      State the name of this tool.

      _____

   (d) State the name of an adhesive used in the assembly of the table.

      _____

   (e) The top was made by gluing strips of wood together as shown.

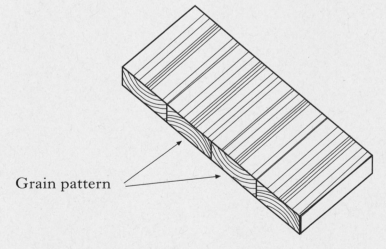

      Grain pattern

      Explain why the grain was arranged in this way.

      _____

DO NOT
WRITE IN
THIS
MARGIN

4. A coat hook made from mild steel is shown.

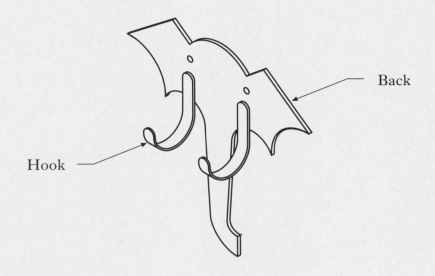

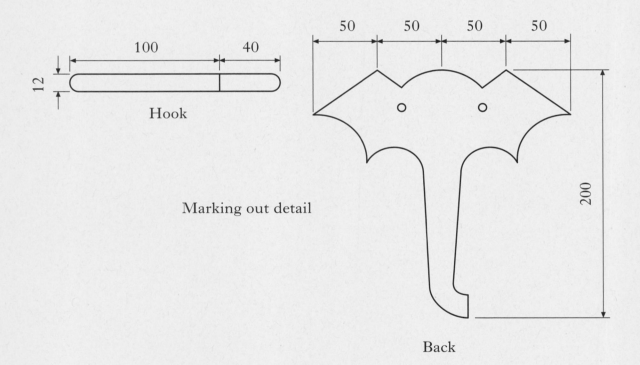

Marking out detail

Back

(*a*) Complete the cutting list for the coat hook.

Part	Number	Length	Breadth	Thickness	Material
Hook			12	1	Mild steel
Back	1		200	2	Mild steel

2
1
0
1
0

DO NOT
WRITE IN
THIS
MARGIN

4. **(continued)**

(b) The two vices shown were used in the manufacture of the coat hook. State the name of each vice.

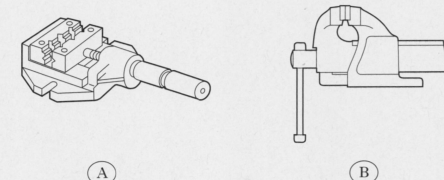

Ⓐ   Ⓑ

(i) Vice Ⓐ _____

(ii) Vice Ⓑ _____

(c) Other than gluing, state **two** methods of joining the hook to the back.

Method 1 _____

Method 2 _____

(d) (i) State a reason for applying a finish to the coat hook.

_____

(ii) State a suitable finish for the coat hook.

_____

[Turn over

1
0
1
0

1
0
1
0

1
0

1
0

DO NOT
WRITE IN
THIS
MARGIN

5. Part of a pupil's revision folder is shown below. Complete the chart by filling in the three blanks.

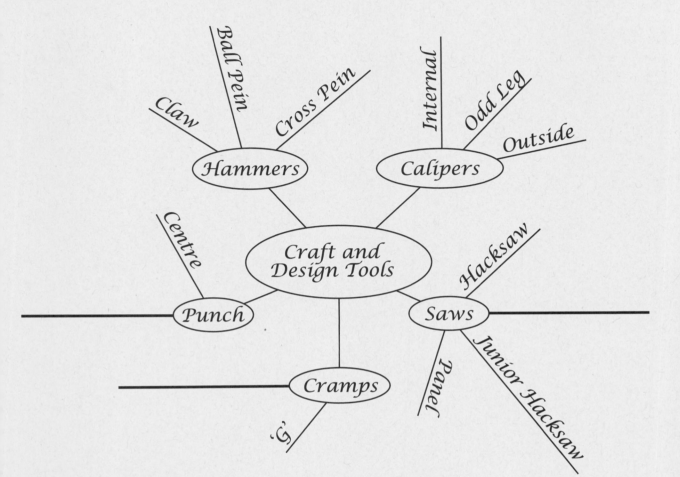

3
2
1
0

DO NOT
WRITE IN
THIS
MARGIN

6. The incomplete research section of a pupil's design folio is shown below.

Material Description

heavy, magnetic
brown coloured
shiny, available in many colours
silver coloured
made up of layers
red coloured

Classification

hardwood
manufactured board
non-ferrous
thermoplastic
softwood
ferrous

Use the lists above to complete the materials table shown below.

Material	Material Description	Classification
Mild steel	heavy, magnetic	ferrous
Plywood		manufactured board
Mahogany	red coloured	
Acrylic		thermoplastic
Copper	brown coloured	

1
0
1
0
1
0
1
0

[Turn over

7. The brief for a doorstop is given below.

> **Brief**
>
> Design and manufacture an attractive device used to keep a door open. It must be capable of being mass produced at an affordable cost.

(*a*) State the part of the brief that refers to:

Economics _____

Aesthetics _____

Function _____

A possible solution to the brief is shown below.

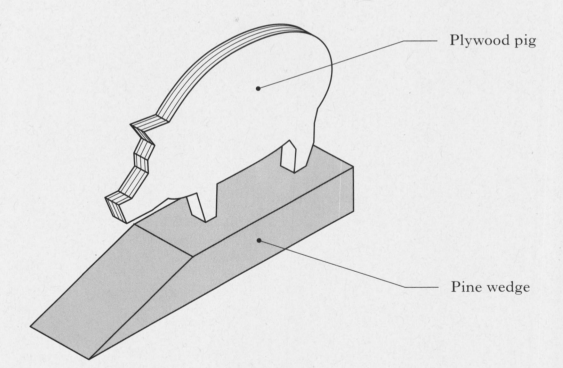

Plywood pig

Pine wedge

(*b*) State a property which makes plywood a suitable choice of material for the pig shape.

_____

(*c*) State an advantage of using a template to mark out the pig shape.

_____

7. **(continued)**

(*d*) State the name of a saw that could be used to cut out the pig shape.

_____

1
0

(*e*) State the name of a suitable abrasive paper that could be used to smooth the edges of the plywood pig.

_____

1
0

(*f*) The pig was joined to the base as shown below.

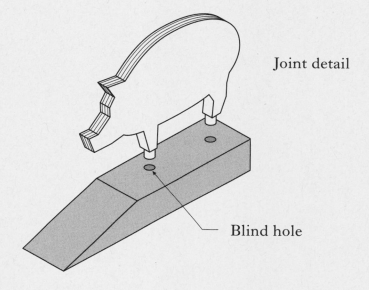

Joint detail

Blind hole

   (i) State the name of this joint.

_____

1
0

  (ii) During the manufacture of the joint, blind holes were drilled.

State what is meant by a blind hole.

_____

1
0

[Turn over for Question 7 (*g*) on *Page fourteen*

DO NOT
WRITE I
THIS
MARGIN

7.   (continued)

(*g*) A prototype door stop is shown below.

Describe **one** design fault evident in the prototype.

_____

1
0

[END OF QUESTION PAPER]

[BLANK PAGE]

FOR OFFICIAL USE

C

Total Mark

0600/403

NATIONAL
QUALIFICATIONS
2006

MONDAY, 8 MAY
2.55 PM – 3.55 PM

CRAFT AND DESIGN
STANDARD GRADE
Credit Level

Fill in these boxes and read what is printed below.

Full name of centre

Town

Forename(s)

Surname

Date of birth

Day Month Year   Scottish candidate number   Number of seat

1 Answer all the questions.

2 Read every question carefully before you answer.

3 Write your answers in the spaces provided.

4 Do **not** write in the margins.

5 All dimensions are given in millimetres.

6 Before leaving the examination room you must give this book to the invigilator. If you do not, you may lose all the marks for this paper.

SCOTTISH
QUALIFICATIONS
AUTHORITY

DO NO
WRITE
THIS
MARGI

ATTEMPT ALL QUESTIONS

1. A pair of pliers is shown below.

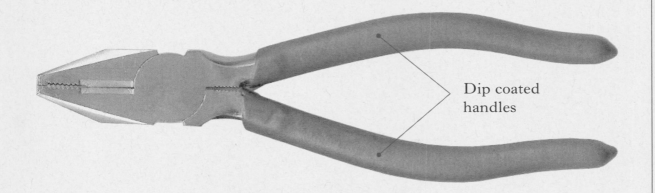

Dip coated
handles

(*a*) During the design of the pliers, reference was made to data sheets of human dimensions.

State the name of this type of data.

_____

1
0

(*b*) The pliers have been designed to be used by adults in the *5th to 95th percentile* range.

Explain what is meant by the term *5th percentile to 95th percentile* range.

Sketches may be used to illustrate your answer.

_____

_____

_____

_____

_____

_____

_____

2
1
0

(*c*) The handles have been dip coated using a thermoplastic.

State what is meant by the term *thermoplastic*.

_____

1
0

DO NOT WRITE IN THIS MARGIN

1. (continued)

(*d*) Complete the sequence of operations for dip coating the handles.

Stage 1 Degrease and clean the metal.

Stage 2 ______________________________ 1 0

Stage 3 ______________________________ 1 0

Stage 4 ______________________________ 1 0

(*e*) State the most likely reason why the plastic coating looked dull and gritty after dip coating.

______________________________ 1 0

(*f*) State **two** reasons why a thermoplastic is a suitable finish for the handles.

(i) ______________________________ 1 0

(ii) ______________________________ 1 0

[Turn over

DO NOT
WRITE IN
THIS
MARGIN

2. A table lamp is shown below.

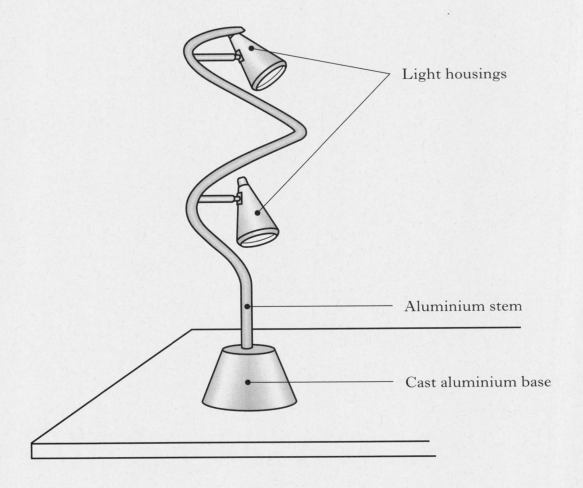

Light housings

Aluminium stem

Cast aluminium base

(*a*)   Market research was carried out during the investigation stage of the design process.

  (i)   Explain the purpose of market research.

_____

1
0

  (ii)   Describe how market research could be carried out.

_____

1
0

2. (continued)

(b) During the design process a model of the lamp was made.

State **two** reasons why modelling is used in the design process.

(i) _____

(ii) _____

(c) The stem was modelled using *malleable* wire.

(i) Explain what is meant by the term *malleable*.

_____

(ii) State the name of a malleable metal suitable for modelling the stem.

_____

(d) In order to cast the aluminium base, a wooden pattern was produced.

wooden
pattern

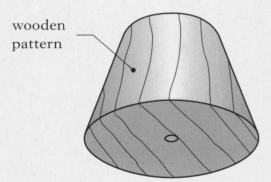

State **two** features of the pattern that would allow it to be easily removed from the moulding sand.

(i) _____

(ii) _____

[Turn over

DO NOT
WRITE IN
THIS
MARGIN

2. (continued)

(e) During the manufacture of the stem it was necessary to *anneal* the aluminium.

(i) State the purpose of *annealing* the aluminium.

_____

(ii) Describe the process of *annealing* aluminium.

_____

_____

_____

_____

(f) Two problems were found during the evaluation of the desk lamp.

Problem 1   The lamp falls over very easily.
Problem 2   The base scratches the surface of the desk.

Describe a design modification that would solve each problem.

(i) Problem 1

_____

_____

(ii) Problem 2

_____

_____

DO NOT
WRITE IN
THIS
MARGIN

3. A baby's cot is shown below.

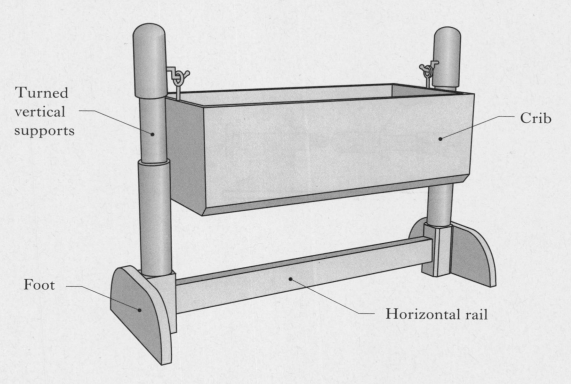

Turned vertical supports

Crib

Foot

Horizontal rail

  (a)   During the design process various techniques were used to generate ideas.

State the name of **two** techniques used by designers to help generate ideas.

    (i) _____

    (ii) _____

1
0
1
0

[Turn over

3. **(continued)**

(*b*)   The vertical supports were turned between centres on a woodwork lathe.

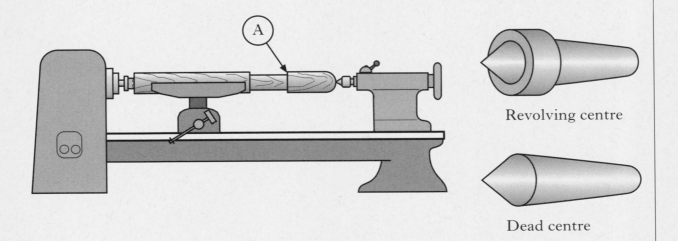

Revolving centre

Dead centre

(i)   State an advantage of using a revolving centre instead of a dead centre.

_____

1
0

(ii)   State the name of the turning tool used to produce the square shoulder shown at (A).

_____

1
0

(iii)   State the name of a tool that could be used to check the diameter of the supports.

_____

1
0

(iv)   State an adjustment that could be made to the woodwork lathe to improve the surface finish of the supports.

_____

1
0

3. **(continued)**

(c)   A sketch of the part assembled cot is shown below.

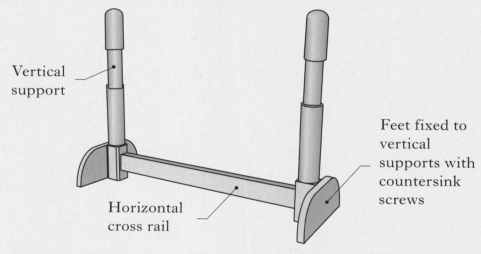

Vertical support

Feet fixed to vertical supports with countersink screws

Horizontal cross rail

Knock down fittings were used to join the horizontal cross rail to the vertical supports.

Explain a benefit of using knock down fittings over a traditional method of joining.

_____

1
0

(d)   The feet of the crib are fixed to vertical supports using countersink screws.

On the diagram below label the following:

(A) Pilot hole   (B) Countersink hole   (C) Clearance hole

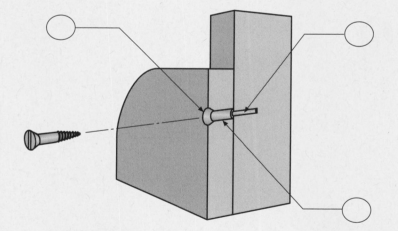

1
0

1
0

1
0

(e)   The designer chose to make the cot from pine.

State why pine is considered a more environmentally friendly material to use than hardwood.

_____

1
0

DO NOT
WRITE IN
THIS
MARGIN

4. A towel rail is shown below.

Assembled towel rail

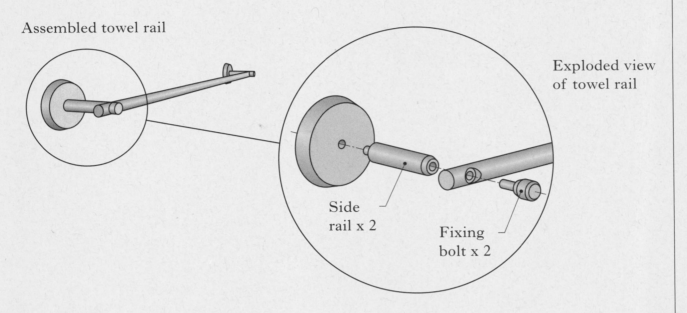

Exploded view
of towel rail

Side
rail x 2

Fixing
bolt x 2

(a) The fixing bolts were manufactured using a metalwork lathe.

State the names of the turning processes shown below.

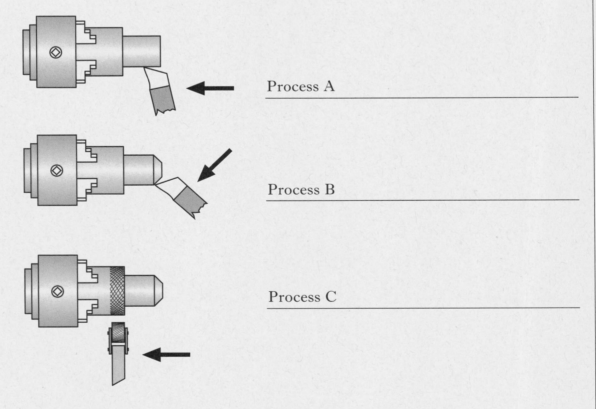

Process A _____

1 0

Process B _____

1 0

Process C _____

1 0

(b) State **two** reasons why a change in lathe speed may be necessary when turning the fixing bolts.

1. _____

1 0

2. _____

1 0

4. (continued)

(c)   The side rail is shown below.

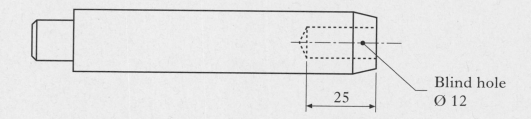

25

Blind hole
Ø 12

The blind hole is to be drilled using a metalwork lathe.   Complete the sequence of operations for drilling the blind hole accurately to a depth of 25 mm.

Stage 1   Face off the end of the bar

Stage 2 _____

_____

Stage 3 _____

_____

Stage 4 _____

_____

(d)   A thread is to be cut in the blind hole.

(i)   State why particular care must be taken when threading a blind hole.

_____

(ii)   State the name of the first tap used when threading the blind hole.

_____

(iii)   State the name of the last tap used when threading the blind hole.

_____

[Turn over

5. A coat hook is shown below.

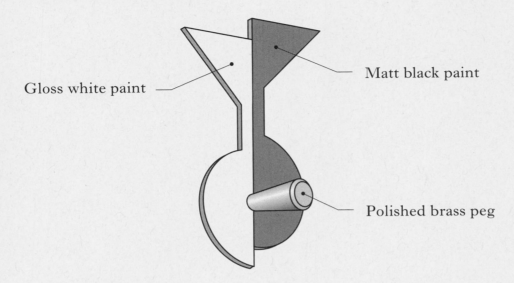

Gloss white paint

Matt black paint

Polished brass peg

(*a*)   (i)   State **two** examples of contrast in the coat hook.

1. _____

2. _____

1
0

1
0

(ii)   State a reason why designers use contrast in design.

_____

1
0

(*b*)   The peg is shown below.

Taper Ⓐ   Ⓑ

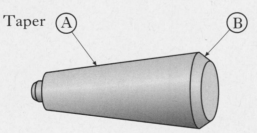

(i)   State a functional reason for the peg being tapered at Ⓐ.

_____

1
0

(ii)   State a reason for removing the corner at Ⓑ.

_____

1
0

(*c*)   The peg is made from brass, a non-ferrous alloy.

State what is meant by:

(i)   Non-ferrous _____

(ii)   An alloy _____

1
0

1
0

DO NOT
WRITE IN
THIS
MARGIN

5. (continued)

The back plate is made from 4 mm thick mild steel.

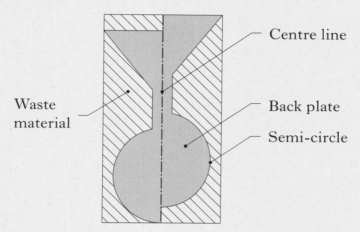

Centre line

Waste material

Back plate

Semi-circle

(d)   Odd leg calipers were used in marking out the shape.

    (i)   Complete the sketch of the odd leg calipers shown below.

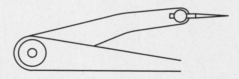

1
0

    (ii)   Describe how the odd leg calipers can be used to find the centre of the blank material without the use of a rule. *Sketches may be used to illustrate your answer.*

_____

_____

_____

_____

_____

_____

_____

2
1
0

(e)   State the name of the tool used to mark the semi-circles.

_____

1
0

(f)   State the name of a suitable hand tool used to remove the waste material from the back plate.

_____

1
0

[Turn over for Question 5 (g), (h) and (i) on Page fourteen

DO NOT
WRITE IN
THIS
MARGIN

5. (continued)

(g)   The back plate is to be painted in two colours.

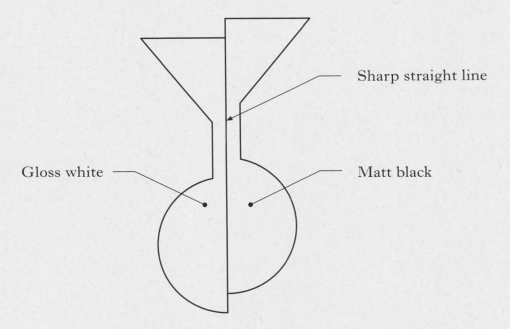

Sharp straight line

Gloss white

Matt black

Describe a method of achieving a sharp straight line between the colours when applying the paint to the back plate.

_____

_____

1
0

(h)   The brass peg is polished then finished with lacquer.

State a reason why this is a suitable finish.

_____

1
0

(i)   Throughout the design process the specification is constantly referred to.

State why a designer would do this.

_____

1
0

[*END OF QUESTION PAPER*]

[BLANK PAGE]

FOR OFFICIAL USE

G

Total

0600/402

| NATIONAL QUALIFICATIONS 2007 | THURSDAY, 10 MAY G/C 1.35 PM – 2.35 PM F/G 2.35 PM – 3.35 PM | CRAFT AND DESIGN STANDARD GRADE General Level |

Fill in these boxes and read what is printed below.

Full name of centre

Town

Forename(s)

Surname

Date of birth
Day Month Year

Scottish candidate number

Number of seat

1 Answer all the questions.

2 Read every question carefully before you answer.

3 Write your answers in the spaces provided.

4 Do **not** write in the margins.

5 All dimensions are given in millimetres.

6 Before leaving the examination room you must give this book to the invigilator. If you do not, you may lose all the marks for this paper.

SCOTTISH QUALIFICATIONS AUTHORITY

©

ATTEMPT ALL QUESTIONS

1. A book stand made from wood is shown below.

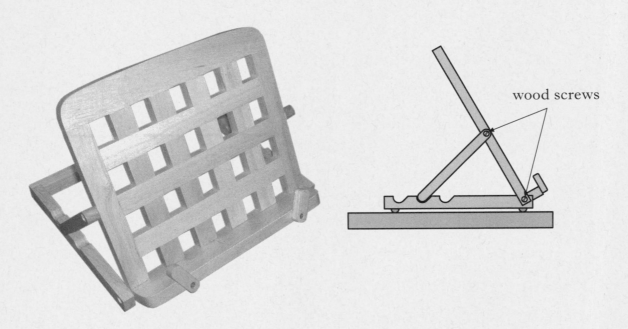

wood screws

(a) State **one** feature of the stand that makes it suitable for use by a range of users.

_____

1
0

(b) The wood joints shown below were used in the manufacture of the book stand. State the name of each joint.

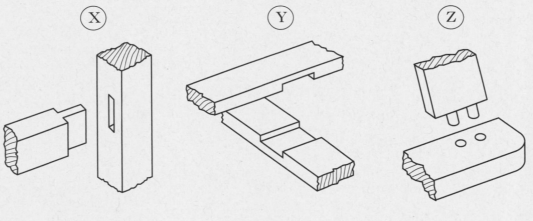

X   Y   Z

Joint (X) _____

Joint (Y) _____

Joint (Z) _____

1
0
1
0
1
0

1.   (continued)

(c)   The tool shown below was used during the manufacture of the book stand.

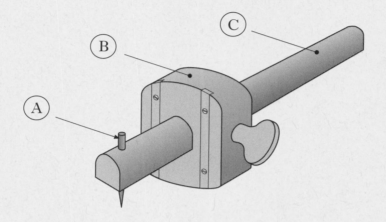

(i)   State the name of this tool.

_____

1
0

(ii)   Select the name of the parts lettered Ⓐ, Ⓑ and Ⓒ from the list below.

Stock   *Spur*   *Stem*   *Thumbscrew*

Ⓐ _____

Ⓑ _____

Ⓒ _____

1
0
1
0
1
0

(d)   The wood screw shown below was used in the manufacture of the book stand.

(i)   State the name of this type of wood screw.

_____

1
0

(ii)   State **one** reason for using a wood screw with this type of head.

_____

1
0

DO NOT
WRITE IN
THIS
MARGIN

2.   A pupil's design for a menu holder is shown below.

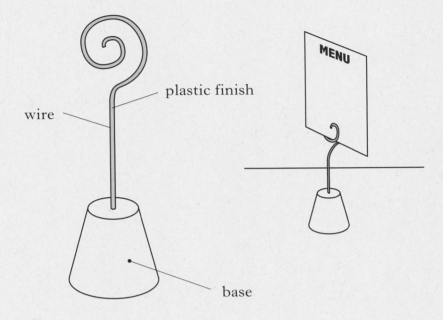

(a)   The base was made from aluminium.

State **one** reason for this choice of material.

_____

1
0

(b)   (i)   The base was made by a process of pouring molten aluminium into a sand mould.

Select the name of this process from the list below.

Forging   Casting   Welding   Turning

Name of process _____

1
0

DO NOT
WRITE IN
THIS
MARGIN

2.   (b) (continued)

A cross-section of the moulding boxes is shown below.

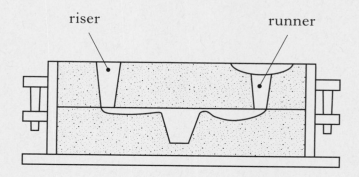

(ii)   State the purpose of the runner and the riser.

Runner_____

Riser   _____

1
0
1
0
0

(c)   A protective plastic finish was applied to the wire.

(i)   State the name of this process.

_____

1
0

(ii)   Several stages in the finishing process are listed in the **wrong** order.

allow metal to cool   place metal in fluidiser   heat metal in oven

clean metal with emery cloth

Arrange the stages in the correct order. The first one has been done for you.

1   Clean metal with emery cloth

2   _____

3   _____

4   _____

1
0
1
0
1
0

[Turn over

DO NOT
WRITE IN
THIS
MARGIN

3.   A pupil's design for a bedside unit is shown below.

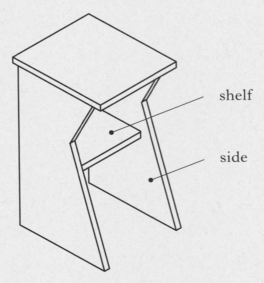

shelf

side

(*a*)   The bedside unit is made from a manufactured board.

(i)   State the name of a suitable manufactured board.

_____

1
0

(ii)   State **one** reason for using a manufactured board.

_____

1
0

(*b*)   The joint shown below was used to join the shelf to the sides.

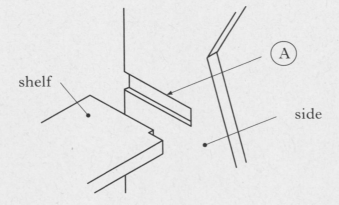

shelf

Ⓐ

side

(i)   State the name of this joint.

_____

1
0

DO NOT
WRITE IN
THIS
MARGIN

3.   **(b) (continued)**

(ii) One stage in the manufacture of Part $\textcircled{A}$ of the joint is given below.

List **three** further stages.

1 mark out joint using try square and pencil.

2 _____

    _____

3 _____

    _____

4 _____

    _____

1
0

1
0

1
0

[Turn over

DO NOT
WRITE IN
THIS
MARGIN

4.   The specification and ideas for an egg holder are shown below.

Specification

•   The holder must hold an egg securely

•   The holder must be easy to clean

•   The holder must have no sharp edges or corners

•   The holder must be stable

•   The holder must be made from one piece of plastic

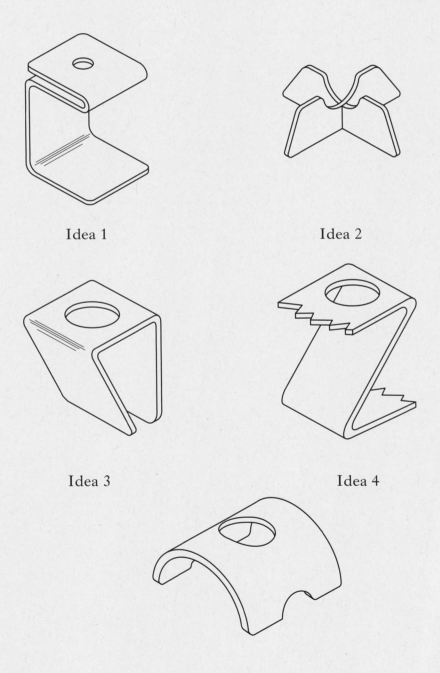

Idea 1   Idea 2

Idea 3   Idea 4

Idea 5

4.   **(continued)**

(*a*)   After evaluation it was agreed that Idea 5 was the only one to meet the specification.

Ideas 1, 2, 3 and 4 did **not** meet the specification.   State the reason why each idea failed.

Idea 1 _____

Idea 2 _____

Idea 3 _____

Idea 4 _____

(*b*)   During the design process eggs were measured.

The callipers shown below were used to measure eggs.

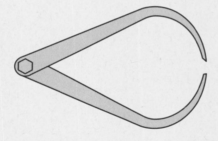

(i)   State the name of these callipers.

_____

(ii)   State the stage in the design process when eggs would be measured.

_____

(*c*)   During the design of the egg holder, models were made.

(i)   State a suitable material for modelling the egg holder.

_____

(ii)   State **one** reason for your choice of material.

_____

DO NOT
WRITE IN
THIS
MARGIN

4.　**(continued)**

(*d*)　The final solution was made from plastic.

State **two** reasons why plastic is a good choice of material.

Reason 1 _____

Reason 2 _____

1
0
1
0

DO NOT
WRITE IN
THIS
MARGIN

5.   A guitar stand made from mild steel is shown below.

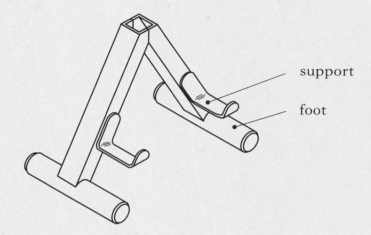

support

foot

(a)   The ends of the feet were turned on a metal lathe.

(i)   State the name of the turning process shown below.

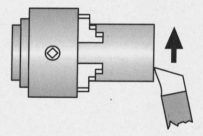

Name of turning process _____

1
0

(ii)   The sharp edges at the ends of each foot were removed as shown below.

State the name of this turning process.

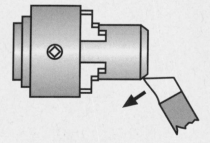

Name of turning process _____

1
0

[**Turn over**

DO NOT
WRITE I
THIS
MARGI

5. **(continued)**

(*b*) Two safety precautions when using a metal lathe are given below.

State **two** further precautions.

1   Wear safety goggles

2   Tie up loose clothing and hair

3   _____

4   _____

1
0
1
0

(*c*) The supports were marked out using the tools shown.

State the name and purpose of each tool.

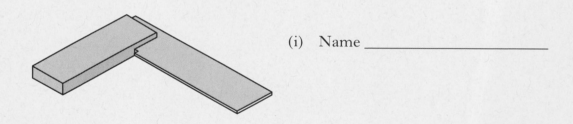

(i)   Name _____

1
0

(ii) Purpose _____

_____

1
0

5.   (c) (continued)

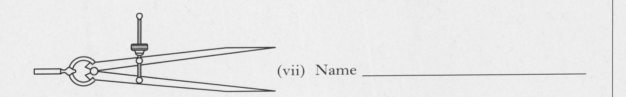

(iii) Name _____

(iv) Purpose_____

_____

(v)   Name _____

(vi) Purpose_____

_____

(vii) Name _____

(viii) Purpose_____

_____

[Turn over

DO NO
WRITE
THIS
MARGI

6. A school enterprise group made thermoplastic photo frames. An example is shown below.

(*a*) State **one** reason for measuring the size of photographs during the design process.

_____

1
0

(*b*) State the name of a suitable thermoplastic for the photo frame.

_____

1
0

(*c*) The photo frame was marked out using a template as shown below.

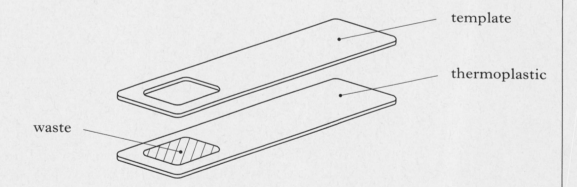

template

thermoplastic

waste

(i) State **one** reason for using a template.

_____

1
0

(ii) Other than a pen or a pencil, state the name of a tool that could be used to mark the waste on the thermoplastic.

_____

1
0

DO NOT
WRITE IN
THIS
MARGIN

6. **(continued)**

(*d*) The machine and tools shown below were used during the manufacture of the picture frame.

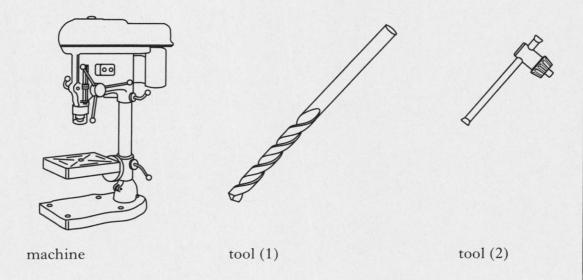

machine   tool (1)   tool (2)

(i) State:

the name of the machine

_____

1
0

the name of tool (1)

_____

1
0

the name of tool (2)

_____

1
0

the use of tool (2).

_____

1
0

(ii) State **one** method that would stop the thermoplastic from cracking when it is drilled.

_____

1
0

[Turn over for Question 6 (*e*), (*f*) and (*g*) on *Page sixteen*

DO NOT
WRITE IN
THIS
MARGIN

6.   **(continued)**

(e)   The waste was removed using the saw shown below.

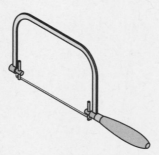

State the name of this saw.

_____

1

0

(f)   Two methods of filing were used when finishing the edges of the thermoplastic.

State the names of these two methods of filing.

Method 1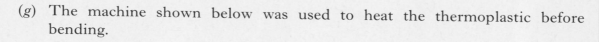

Method 2 _____

1

0

1

0

(g)   The machine shown below was used to heat the thermoplastic before bending.

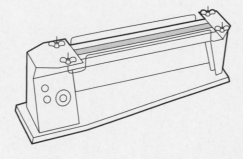

(i)   State the name of this machine.

_____

1

0

(ii)   State what would happen to the thermoplastic if it was not hot enough before bending.

_____

1

0

[END OF QUESTION PAPER]

STANDARD GRADE | CREDIT

2007

[BLANK PAGE]

FOR OFFICIAL USE

C

Total Mark

0600/403

NATIONAL
QUALIFICATIONS
2007

THURSDAY, 10 MAY
2.55 PM – 3.55 PM

CRAFT AND DESIGN
STANDARD GRADE
Credit Level

Fill in these boxes and read what is printed below.

Full name of centre

Town

Forename(s)

Surname

Date of birth
   Day   Month   Year   Scottish candidate number   Number of seat

1   Answer all the questions.

2   Read every question carefully before you answer.

3   Write your answers in the spaces provided.

4   Do **not** write in the margins.

5   All dimensions are given in millimetres.

6   Before leaving the examination room you must give this book to the invigilator. If you do not, you may lose all the marks for this paper.

SCOTTISH
QUALIFICATIONS
AUTHORITY

©

ATTEMPT ALL QUESTIONS

DO NOT
WRITE IN
THIS
MARGIN

1. A wall light is shown.

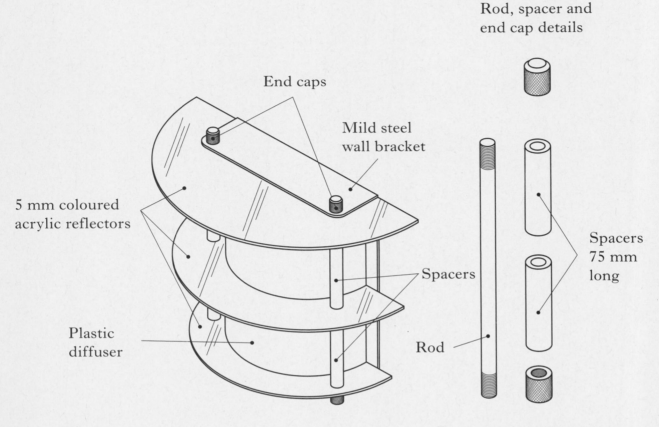

Rod, spacer and
end cap details

End caps

Mild steel
wall bracket

5 mm coloured
acrylic reflectors

Spacers

Spacers
75 mm
long

Plastic
diffuser

Rod

Material Aluminium

(*a*) (i) Colour was an area of aesthetics investigated during the design of the wall light.

State **two** further areas of aesthetics that may have been considered during the design of the wall light.

1 _____

2 _____

(ii) Materials were also investigated during the design of the wall light.

State **two** reasons why the choice of material is important.

1 _____

2 _____

1
0
1
0

1
0
1
0

1. (continued)

(b) "The bulb must be easy to change" appeared in the specification for the wall light.

State the design factor being considered to ensure that the bulb can be easily changed.

_____

10

(c) The three acrylic reflectors were drilled to allow the rods and spacers to be fitted. Describe a method of ensuring that the holes in the acrylic reflectors line up.

_____

_____

10

(d) The mild steel for the wall bracket was marked out as shown.

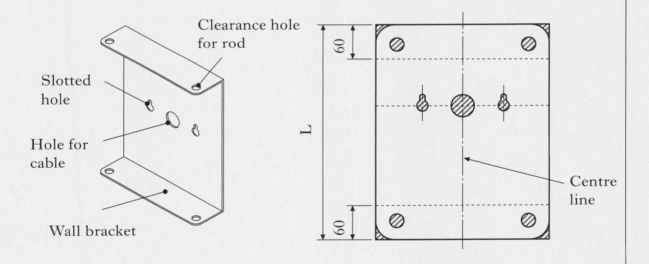

(i) Mild steel is a ferrous metal.

State what is meant by a ferrous metal.

_____

10

(ii) The wall bracket holds three acrylic reflectors and two spacers.

State the total length (L) of the material required for the wall bracket.

Total length (L) _____

10

DO NOT
WRITE IN
THIS
MARGIN

1. (d) (continued)

(iii) A centre line was marked on the material for the wall bracket. Describe how odd leg callipers can be used to scribe a centre line without the use of a ruler. *Sketches may be used to illustrate your answer.*

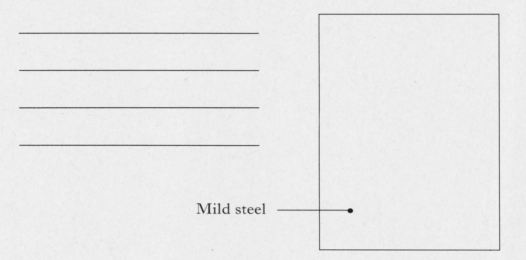

Mild steel

2
1
0

(e) (i) The mild steel was drilled.

State a reason why the metal was centre punched before drilling.

1
0

(ii) State a reason for the slotted holes in the wall bracket.

1
0

(f) (i) The end caps were faced off using a metal lathe.

State **one** fault that would result in a small "pip" forming on the cap during turning.

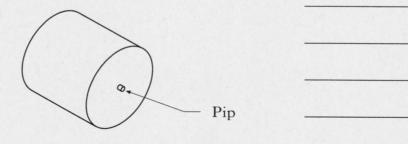

Pip

1
0

1. (f)   (continued)

(ii)   During the manufacture of the end caps the tool shown below was used.

State the name of this tool.

_____

State the purpose of this tool.

_____

(iii)   A metal lathe was used when drilling a blind hole in each end cap.

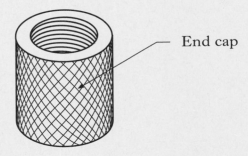

End cap

Describe a method of ensuring the depth of the blind holes is 30 mm.

_____

_____

**1
0**

**1
0**

**1
0**

[Turn over

DO NO
WRITE
THIS
MARGI

1. (continued)

(g) (i) Taps were used to thread the blind holes.

State the name of the last tap used when threading a blind hole.

_____

1
0

(ii) The tool shown below was used to cut an external thread on the rod.

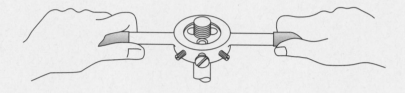

State the name of this tool.

_____

1
0

(iii) The thread was found to be a tight fit. Describe how to adjust this tool to ensure a good fitting thread.

_____

_____

_____

2
1
0

(h) The end caps were knurled.

State an adjustment to the speed of the metal lathe that may be necessary prior to knurling.

_____

1
0

2. A hand held toy is shown.

(*a*)   The toy was made from a light coloured, close grained hardwood.

State the name of a suitable hardwood.

1
0

(*b*)   The four wheels were made using the wood lathe as shown.

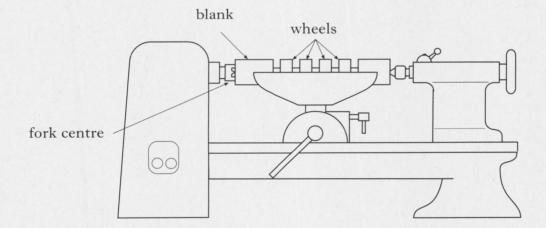

(i)   State a reason why the blank is longer than the combined width of the four wheels.

1
0

[Turn over

DO NOT
WRITE IN
THIS
MARGIN

2. (b)   (continued)

(ii)   On the sketch show how the end of the blank is prepared for fixing to the fork centre.

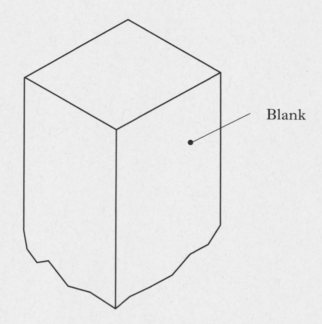

Blank

1
0

(iii)   State the name of **two** turning tools used during the manufacture of the wheels.

Tool 1 _____

Tool 2 _____

1
0
1
0

(iv)   The following tool was used during the manufacture of the wheels.

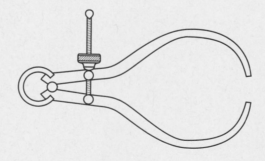

State the name of this tool and describe its purpose.

Name_____

Purpose_____

1
0
1
0

2. (b)   (continued)

(v) The wheels were sanded before removal from the wood lathe. State **two** adjustments that should be carried out before sanding.

1 _____

2 _____

1
0
1
0

(c) The three holes listed were drilled in preparation for fixing the wheels to the body using wood screws.

Countersink   **Pilot**   **Clearance**

Label the holes on the sketch using the list above.

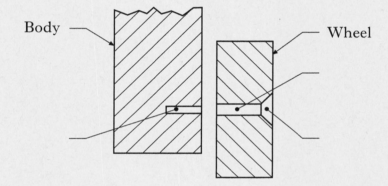

Body

Wheel

3
2
1
0

[Turn over

DO NOT
WRITE IN
THIS
MARGIN

3. A pupil's design for a chair is shown.

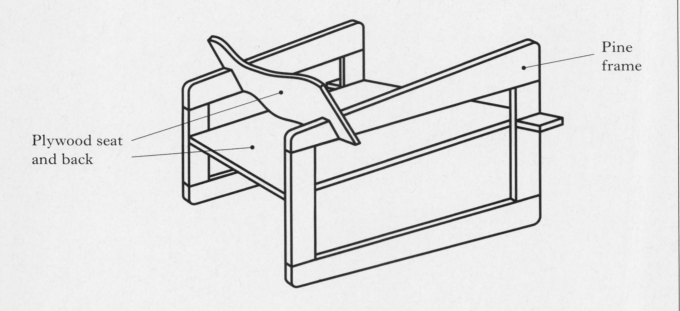

Pine
frame

Plywood seat
and back

(a) (i) During the design of the chair a scale model was made.

State **two** reasons for producing a scale model.

Reason 1 _____

_____

Reason 2 _____

_____

1
0

1
0

(ii) An ergonome was used during the design of the chair.

State what is meant by *an ergonome*.

_____

_____

1
0

(b) (i) Pine and hardwoods were considered for the frame of the chair. Explain why the use of pine is considered more environmentally friendly than the use of a hardwood.

_____

_____

1
0

3. **(*b*)** **(continued)**

Plywood was used for the seat and the back of the chair.

(ii) Describe the constructional feature that gives plywood its strength.

Sketches may be used to illustrate your answer.

_____

_____

_____

_____

1
0

(*c*)   (i)   The tool shown below was used in the manufacture of the chair.

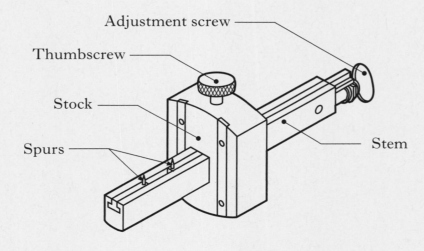

Adjustment screw

Thumbscrew

Stock

Spurs

Stem

State the name of the tool.

Tool _____

1
0

(ii) Describe **two** adjustments that could be made to this tool.

1 _____

_____

1
0

2 _____

_____

1
0

[Turn over

3. (continued)

(d)   The fixing shown below was used during the manufacture of the chair.

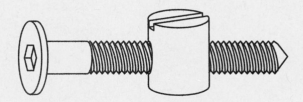

State the name of this type of fixing.

_____

1
0

(e)   The taper on the arm was formed using a plane.

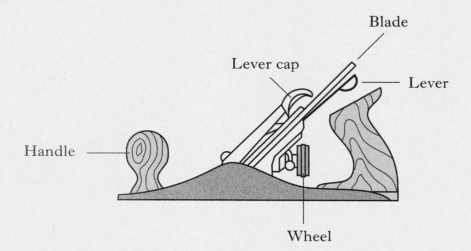

Describe how the plane can be adjusted to:

(i)   ensure that the blade is level

_____

_____

1
0

(ii)   change the depth of cut

_____

_____

1
0

DO NOT
WRITE IN
THIS
MARGIN

3. *(e)* **(continued)**

(iii) State a reason why the taper on the arm was planed in the direction shown.

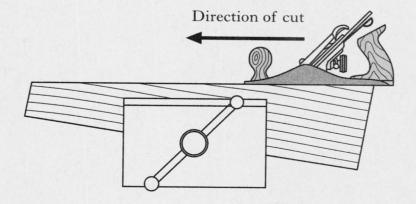

Direction of cut

Reason _____

_____

1
0

[Turn over

DO NOT
WRITE IN
THIS
MARGIN

4. Bathroom scales are shown.

Toughened
glass

Digital display

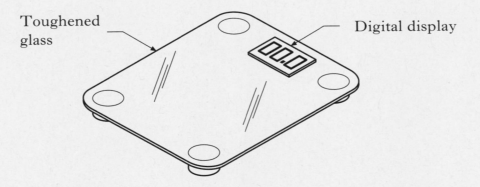

(a)   **Ergonomics** was investigated during the design of the scales.

State what is meant by the term *ergonomics*.

_____

_____

1
0

(b)   (i)   The following table was referred to during the design of the scales.

	Adult males			Adult females		
	5th % ile	50th % ile	95th % ile	5th % ile	50th % ile	95th % ile
Foot length	240	260	285	215	235	255
Foot width	85	95	110	80	90	100

State the name of this type of data.

_____

1
0

DO NOT WRITE IN THIS MARGIN

4. (*b*) (continued)

(ii) This table refers to 5th, 50th and 95th percentiles.

State what is meant by:

5th percentile

____

____ **1 0**

50th percentile

____

____ **1 0**

(*c*) The 95th percentile sizes were considered to be important.

State why these are important.

____

____ **1 0**

[Turn over

DO NOT WRITE IN THIS MARGIN

5. A radio controlled racing car is shown below.

Polystyrene body shell

(*a*) (i) The body shell was made from polystyrene, a type of thermoplastic.

State what is meant by the term *thermoplastic*.

_____

_____

1 0

(ii) Acrylic was rejected as a possible material for the body shell.

State a reason why acrylic was considered an unsuitable material.

_____

1 0

(*b*) (i) The body shell was manufactured using the machine shown below.

State the name of this machine.

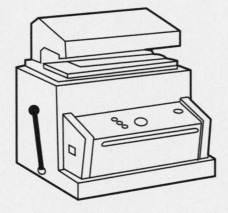

Name_____

1 0

5. (b)   (continued)

(ii) Some stages in the manufacture of the body shell are listed below in the wrong order.

- when cool, unclamp the plastic and remove the pattern

- heat the plastic until soft

- switch on the pump and suck out the air

- remove the heat and raise the pattern into the soft plastic

Using the stages listed above, complete the following sequence of operations.

Sequence of operations

1 Place the pattern in the machine and clamp the plastic

2 _____

3 _____

4 _____

5 _____

6 Trim off excess plastic

4
3
2
1
0

[Turn over

DO NOT
WRITE IN
THIS
MARGIN

5. (continued)

(*c*)   The pattern used during the manufacture of the body shell is shown below.

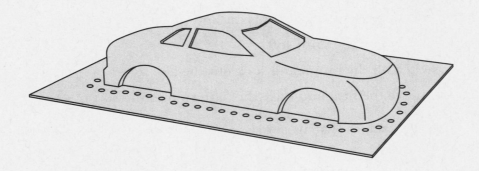

Sloping sides, rounded corners and small holes are all features of the pattern.

State a reason for each feature.

(i)   Sloping sides

_____

_____

1
0

(ii)   Rounded corners

_____

_____

1
0

(iii)   Small holes

_____

_____

1
0

[END OF QUESTION PAPER]

STANDARD GRADE | GENERAL

2008

[BLANK PAGE]

FOR OFFICIAL USE

G

Total

0600/402

NATIONAL
QUALIFICATIONS
2008

WEDNESDAY, 14 MAY
10.20 AM –11.20 AM

CRAFT AND DESIGN
STANDARD GRADE
General Level

Fill in these boxes and read what is printed below.

Full name of centre

Town

Forename(s)

Surname

Date of birth
Day Month Year

Scottish candidate number

Number of seat

1 Answer all the questions.

2 Read every question carefully before you answer.

3 Write your answers in the spaces provided.

4 Do **not** write in the margins.

5 All dimensions are given in millimetres.

6 Before leaving the examination room you must give this book to the invigilator. If you do not, you may lose all the marks for this paper.

DO NOT
WRITE I[
THIS
MARGIN

ATTEMPT ALL QUESTIONS

1.   A child's game is shown below.

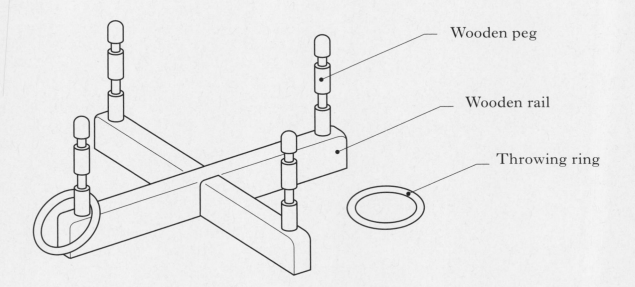

Wooden peg

Wooden rail

Throwing ring

(a)   The rails and pegs are to be made of a hardwood.
State the name of a suitable hardwood.

beach

1
0

(b)   The joint shown below was used in the manufacture of the game.

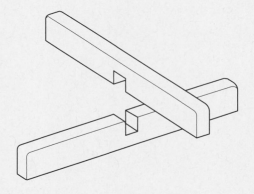

State the name of this joint.

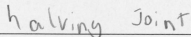

halving joint

1
0

1.   **(continued)**

(*c*)   The following tools were used in the manufacture of the joint.
State the name of each tool.

(i)

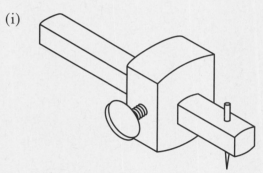

Tool name   *Mortle and Tennon*

1
0

(ii)

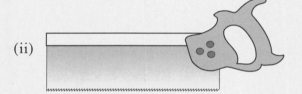

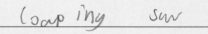

Tool name   *Coaping saw*

1
0

(*d*)   A wooden peg is shown below.

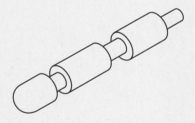

State the name of the machine used to manufacture the peg.

Wood lathe

1
0

[Turn over

DO NOT
WRITE I
THIS
MARGII

1. (continued)

(*e*)   The tools shown below were used when manufacturing the peg.
State the names of these tools.

(i)

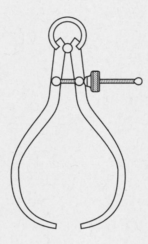

Tool name   _____outside calipers_____

1
0

(ii)

Tool name   _____

1
0

2. A design for a chair is shown below.

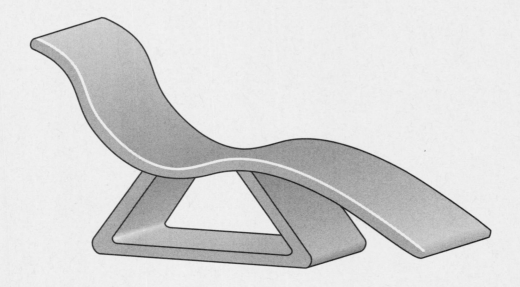

During the design process the following materials were researched.

Pine   Plywood   Mild steel   Aluminium   Acrylic   Oak   Copper

Using the materials list complete the table below.

Material	Classification	Properties
mild steel	Ferrous metal	Strong, magnetic, rusts
Ply wood	Manufactured board	Strong, multi-layered board available in large sheets
aluminium	Non ferrous metal	Lightweight, silver coloured
acrylic	Thermoplastic	Available in many colours, can be heated and shaped
Pine	Softwood	Yellowish red coloured wood

1
0

1
0

1
0

1
0

1
0

[Turn over

DO NOT
WRITE I
THIS
MARGI

3.   A school notice board is shown below.

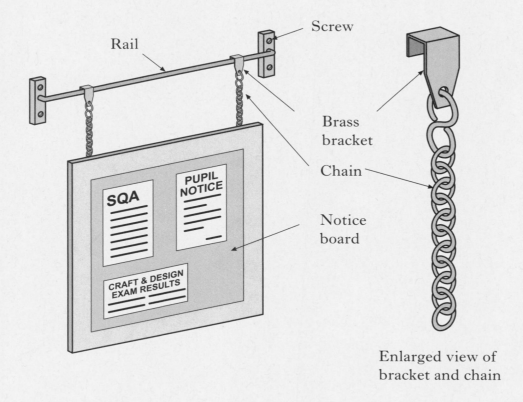

Enlarged view of
bracket and chain

(a)   A statement which appeared in the specification for the notice board is given below.

• It must accommodate a range of notice board sizes.

List **two** other statements that could appear in the design specification.

(i)   _notices must be Readable_

(ii)   _must look good_

1
0
1
0

(b)   The rail is fixed to the wall using the wood screw shown below.

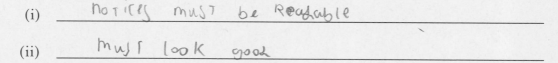

State the name of this type of wood screw.

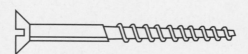

1
0

3.   **(continued)**

During the manufacture of the bracket, the brass was marked out as shown below.

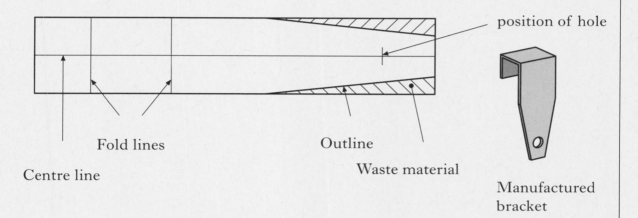

position of hole

Fold lines

Centre line

Outline

Waste material

Manufactured bracket

(c)   A template was used to mark the outline of the bracket.
State **two** advantages of using a template.

Advantage 1 ___IT is neater_____

_____

Advantage 2 ___you can make several____
_The same_____

(d)   Complete the sequence of operations for the manufacture of the bracket.

Stage	Operation	Tool needed
1	Mark outline of the bracket	Scriber
2	*Mark hole for Drill*	Centre punch
3	Mark centre line parallel to edge	*marking gauge*
4	*Cut The edge*	Hacksaw
5	Smooth edges of bracket	*emery paper*
6	*bend on fold lines*	Bending bars
7	Brush	Apply a finish to the metal

1
0

1
0

1
0

1
0

1
0

1
0

1
0

4.   A trophy is shown below.

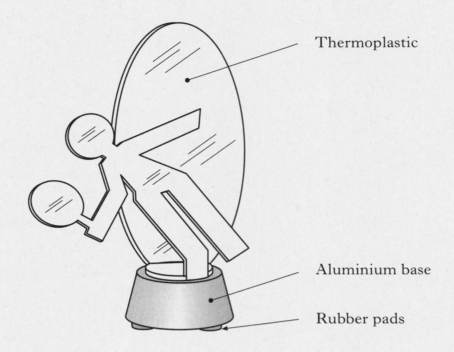

Thermoplastic

Aluminium base

Rubber pads

(*a*)   The process of sand casting was used to manufacture the aluminium base.

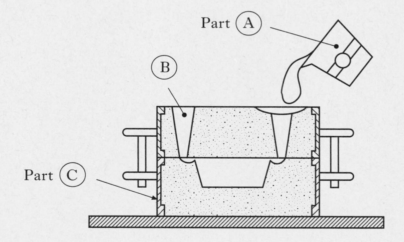

Part (A)

(B)

Part (C)

Some terms relating to the casting process are given below.

Runner   Crucible   Riser   Drag   Moulding Sand

Using these terms, state the name of:

(i)   Part (A) _____Crucible_____

(ii)   The opening at (B) ____Riser_____

(iii)   Part (C) _____Drag_____

1
0
1
0
1
0

4.   (continued)

(b)   State a reason why the rubber pads were fitted to the aluminium base.

So The base Dindnt scratch The surface

**1
0**

The thermoplastic shape is shown below.

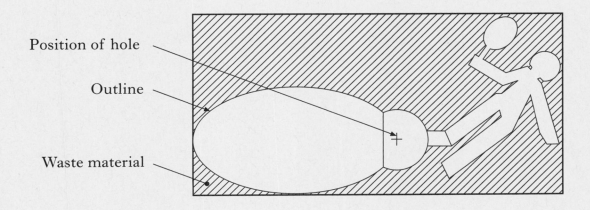

Position of hole

Outline

Waste material

(c)   State the name of a hand tool that could be used to cut out the curved shapes in the thermoplastic.

Coaping saw

**1
0**

(d)   A pedestal drill was used during manufacture.

(i)   State a safety check that should be made to the machine before switching it on.

That The Drillbit is secure

**1
0**

(ii)   State a method that could be used to prevent the plastic from cracking when drilling.

Drilling IT in slow Then Remove and continue This Till Done

**1
0**

[Turn over

DO NOT
WRITE IN
THIS
MARGIN

4.   **(continued)**

   (*e*)   The machine shown below was used during manufacture of the trophy.

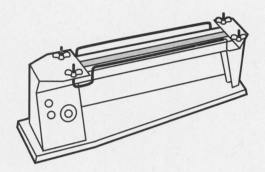

   (i)   State the name of this machine.

   STrip heater

   1
   0

   (ii)   Other than eye protection state a safety precaution that should be followed when using this machine.

   No loose clothing

   1
   0

5.   A designer has been asked to develop a new pair of sunglasses.

During the analysis the designer considered the following design factors.

Ergonomics   Economics   Safety   Aesthetics   Function

Using each design factor once, complete the diagram below.

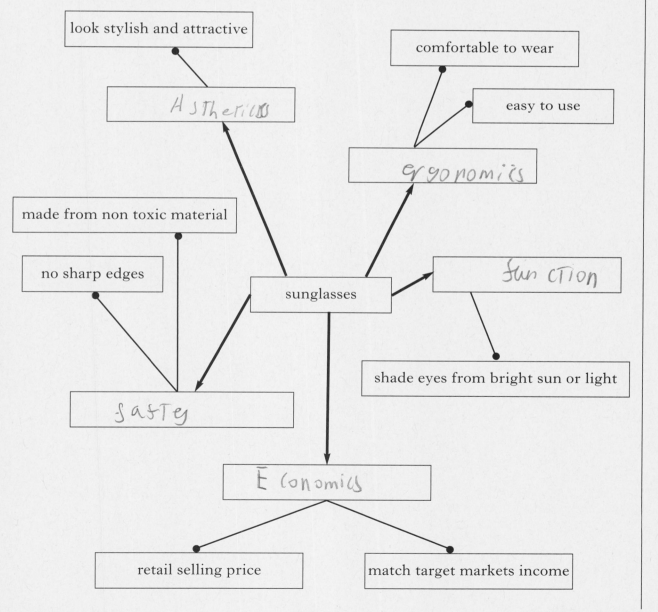

look stylish and attractive

Aﬆhetics

comfortable to wear

easy to use

ergonomics

made from non toxic material

no sharp edges

sunglasses

funCTion

shade eyes from bright sun or light

Safﬆy

Economics

retail selling price

match target markets income

1 0

1 0

1 0

1 0

1 0

DO NO'
WRITE
THIS
MARGI

6.   A covered sand pit table for a nursery is shown below.

Assembled view

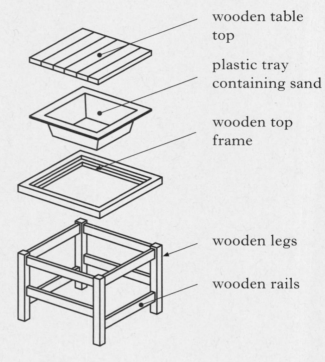

wooden table top

plastic tray containing sand

wooden top frame

wooden legs

wooden rails

Exploded view

(*a*)   The joint shown was used in the manufacture of the table.

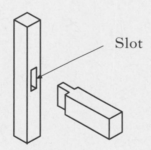

Slot

(i)   State the name of this joint. Mortice and Tenon

1
0

The chisel shown below was used in the manufacture of the joint.

(ii)   State the name of this type of chisel. beril edge

1
0

(iii)   Describe how to ensure that the slot in the leg is cut to the correct depth.

1
0

DO NOT
WRITE IN
THIS
MARGIN

6.   (continued)

(*b*)   State the name of a white coloured wood glue used in the assembly of the wooden table.

PVA

1
0

(*c*)   The table top is made by joining strips of pine together and holding them as shown below.

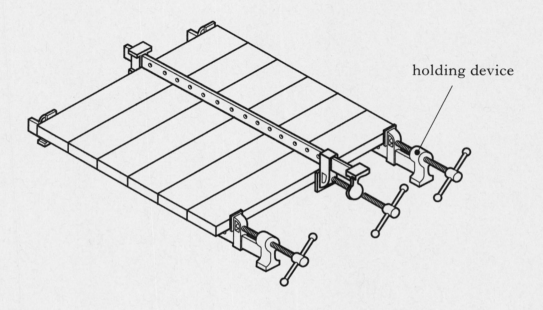

holding device

(i)   State the name of the holding device.

Sash clamps

1
0

(ii)   State a reason for placing one of the holding devices on top.

so the middle Dosnt bend

1
0

(iii)   The edge of the pine was damaged when the holding device was tightened. State how this damage could be avoided.

Small Peile of Scap Wood between edge and holding Devie

1
0

[Turn over

6.   (continued)

(*d*)   The top frame is shown below.

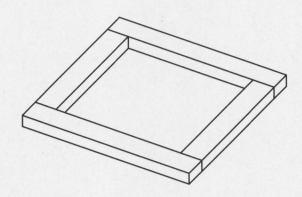

State **two** methods of checking if the top frame is "square".

Method 1 _Try Square_

Method 2 _all_

1
0
1
0

(*e*)   State a suitable finish that could be applied to show the natural grain of the wood.

Varnish

1
0

(*f*)   The plastic tray was shaped using the machine shown below.

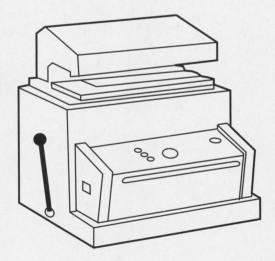

State the name of this machine.

Vacume former

1
0

6. **(continued)**

(g) The pattern shown below was used during the manufacture of the tray.

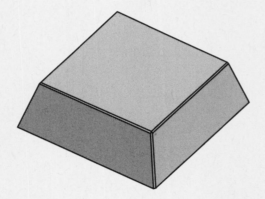

Heavy   Rounded edges   Tapered edges   Wooden

From the list above select the feature of the pattern that would:

(i) prevent tears occurring in the thermoplastic

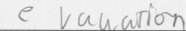 Rounded

1
0

(ii) help with the removal of the tray from the pattern after shaping.

Tapered

1
0

(h) At the end of the manufacture the designer tested the table against the specification. State the name of this stage in the design process.

evaluation

1
0

[Turn over

7.   A shelf unit is shown below.

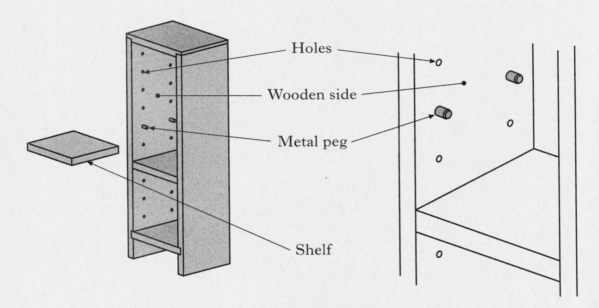

Enlarged interior view of unit

(*a*)   (i)   Holes for the pegs were drilled in the sides.
State a reason why there are more holes than pegs.

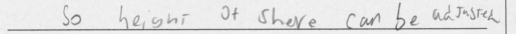

So height of shere can be adjusten

**1
0**

(ii)   The sketch below shows a side of the shelf unit with a hole drilled
part way through.

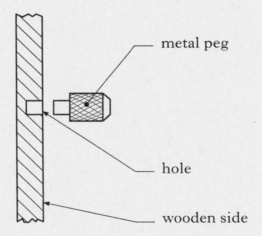

State the name of this type of hole.

_____

**1
0**

DO NOT
WRITE IN
THIS
MARGIN

7.   **(continued)**

(*b*)   The joints shown below were used in the manufacture of the shelf unit.
State the name of these joints.

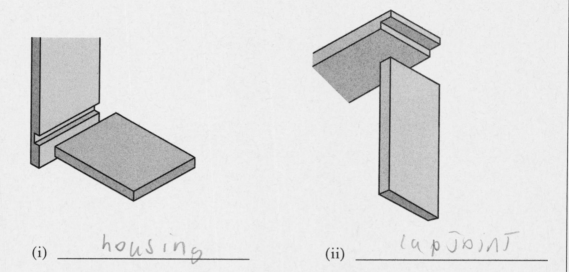

(i) _____housing_____   (ii) _____lap joint_____

One of the metal pegs is shown below.

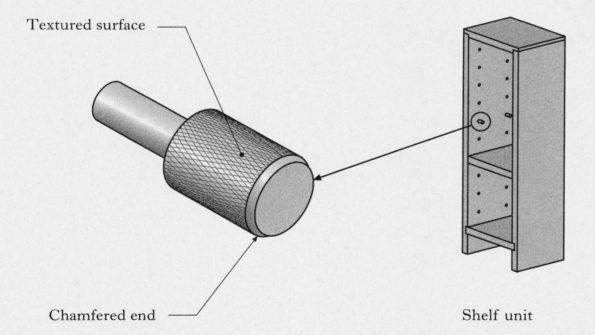

Textured surface

Chamfered end   Shelf unit

Enlarged view of metal peg

2
1
0

[Turn over

DO NOT
WRITE IN
THIS
MARGIN

7.   (continued)

(c)   State a reason for the chamfer on the end of the peg.

So the shelve Dosnt slip

1
0

(d)   State a functional reason for the textured surface on the peg.

So shekve Dosnt slip

1
0

(e)   (i)   The machine shown below was used to manufacture the pegs.
State the name of the machine shown below.

1
0

(ii)   Using the list below state the names of parts (A) (B) and (C).

Chuck   Headstock   Tailstock   Saddle   Toolpost

Part (A)   Part (B)   Part (C)

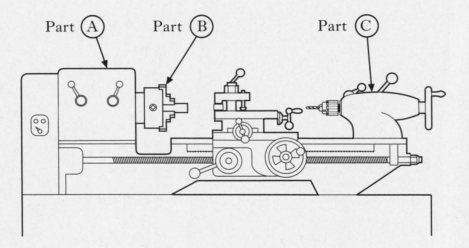

Part (A)   head Stock

1
0

Part (B)   Chuck

1
0

Part (C)   Tail Stock

1
0

[END OF QUESTION PAPER]

STANDARD GRADE | CREDIT

2008

[BLANK PAGE]

FOR OFFICIAL USE

C

Total
Mark

0600/403

NATIONAL
QUALIFICATIONS
2008

WEDNESDAY, 14 MAY
1.00 PM – 2.00 PM

CRAFT AND DESIGN
STANDARD GRADE
Credit Level

Fill in these boxes and read what is printed below.

Full name of centre

Town

Forename(s)

Surname

Date of birth

Day   Month   Year   Scottish candidate number   Number of seat

1 Answer all the questions.

2 Read every question carefully before you answer.

3 Write your answers in the spaces provided.

4 Do **not** write in the margins.

5 All dimensions are given in millimetres.

6 Before leaving the examination room you must give this book to the invigilator. If you do not, you may lose all the marks for this paper.

DO NOT
WRITE IN
THIS
MARGIN

ATTEMPT ALL QUESTIONS

1. A TV unit made from MDF is shown below.

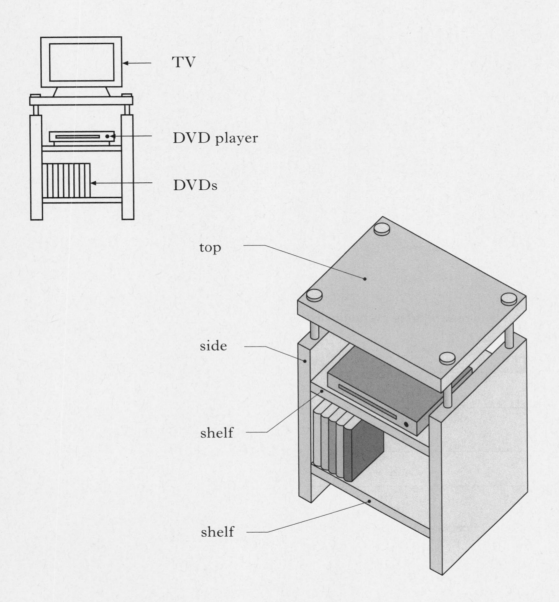

(a) Materials were investigated during the design of the unit.

State **two** further design issues that could be investigated.

(i) _____

(ii) _____

1
0

1
0

DO NOT
WRITE IN
THIS
MARGIN

1. (continued)

(b)   A butt joint was considered for the unit as shown below.

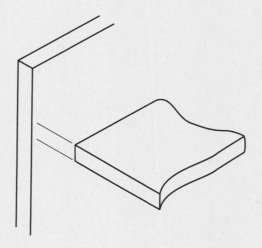

State a reason why this joint was rejected.

_____

1
0

(c)   The joint shown below was used to join the shelves to the sides.

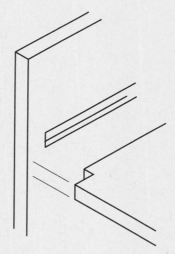

(i)   State the name of this joint.

_____

1
0

(ii)   State an aesthetic reason for using this joint.

_____

1
0

DO NOT
WRITE I
THIS
MARGIN

1. **(continued)**

   (*d*)   A hand router was used to finish the bottom of the joint.

   (i)   With reference to the sketch below, describe how you would set this tool to finish the joint to a depth of 10 mm.

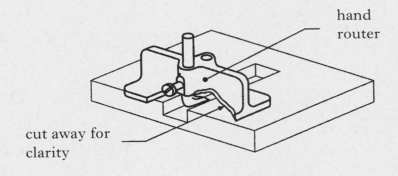

hand
router

cut away for
clarity

_____

_____

_____

2
1
0

   (ii)   State **one** reason why a hand router, rather than a chisel, would be more suitable for "finishing" the bottom of the joint.

_____

1
0

2. The office chair shown below was designed with ergonomics in mind.

(a) (i) State the meaning of the term "ergonomics".

_____

10

(ii) An ergonome was used during the design of the chair.

Describe an "ergonome".

_____

10

(iii) State the purpose of an ergonome.

_____

10

(iv) State **one** ergonomic feature of the chair.

_____

10

(b) The chair has been designed to be used by adults in the 5th to 95th percentile range.

(i) State the percentile used when deciding how wide the back of the chair should be.

_____

10

(ii) State a reason for your answer.

_____

10

[Turn over

DO NOT
WRITE I
THIS
MARGIN

3. A metal gate is shown below.

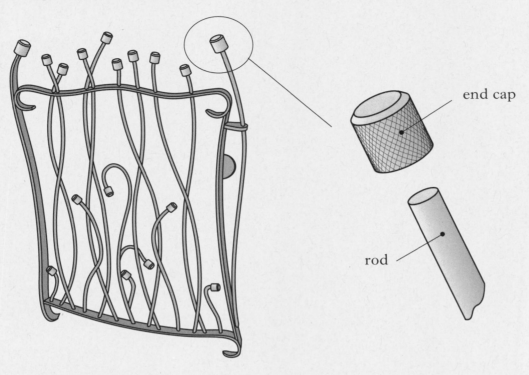

end cap

rod

(a) The end caps were manufactured using a metal lathe.

(i) State the names of the turning processes shown below.

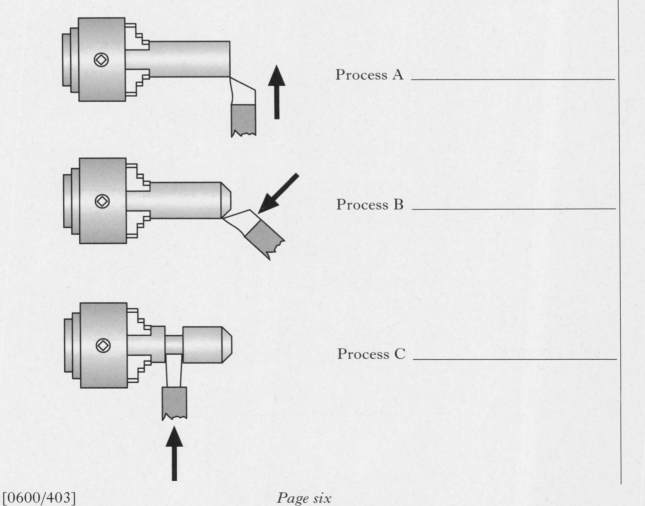

Process A _____

Process B _____

Process C _____

1
0

1
0

1
0

3. (a)   (continued)

(ii)   State **two** reasons why a change in lathe speed may be necessary when turning metal.

1 _____

2 _____

(b)   One end of each rod is threaded.

(i)   State the diameter of rod required for an M6 thread to be cut.

_____

_____

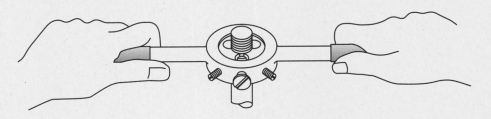

(ii)   State how the end of the rod should be prepared before threading.

_____

_____

(iii)   State the name of the tool used to cut the thread on the end of the rod.

_____

(iv)   State **two** procedures that would ensure a high quality thread is cut.

1 _____

2 _____

(v)   The thread between the end cap and the rod was found to be a tight fit.

Describe an adjustment that could be made to the tool to ensure a good fitting thread.

_____

_____

1
0
1
0

1
0

1
0

1
0

1
0
1
0

2
1
0

4. A pupil's design for a table is shown below.

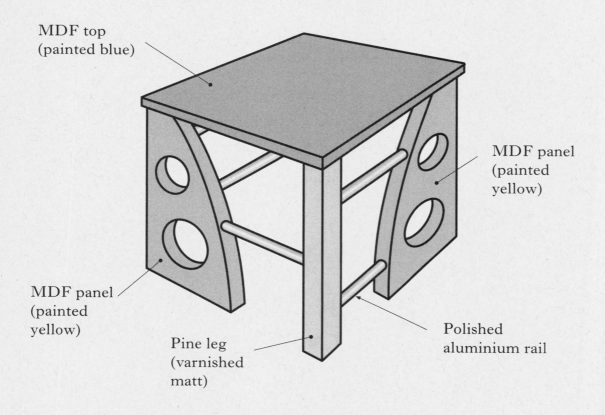

MDF top
(painted blue)

MDF panel
(painted
yellow)

MDF panel
(painted
yellow)

Pine leg
(varnished
matt)

Polished
aluminium rail

(a) The pupil used the theme of "architecture" to help generate ideas.

State another method used to generate ideas.

_____

1
0

(b) The target market was investigated during the design of the table.

State what is meant by the "target market".

_____

1
0

(c) Aesthetics was considered during the design of the table.

Contrast is one aspect of aesthetics.

(i) State **two** examples of contrast used in the design of the table.

1 _____

1
0

2 _____

1
0

DO NOT WRITE IN THIS MARGIN

4. (c) **(continued)**

(ii) State a reason why designers use contrast in design.

____ **1 0**

(*d*) A scale model of the table was made.

(i) State **two** reasons for making a scale model.

Reason 1 ________________________________ **1 0**

Reason 2 ________________________________ **1 0**

(ii) State a suitable material that could have been used to make the scale model.

____ **1 0**

(*e*) A working drawing was produced.

State **two** pieces of information that would be found on a working drawing.

1 ____ **1 0**

2 ____ **1 0**

[Turn over

DO NOT WRITE IN THIS MARGIN

5. A clock is shown below.

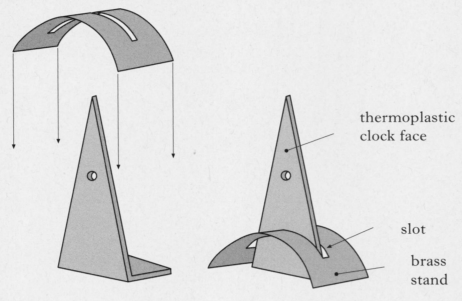

(*a*)   The stand is made from brass sheet. Brass is an alloy.

State the meaning of the term "alloy".

_____

(*b*)   Odd-leg callipers were used to mark the centre line of the slot on the brass sheet as shown below.

Describe a method of setting the odd-leg callipers to half the width of the brass sheet without the use of a rule. Sketches may be used to illustrate your answer.

_____

_____

_____

_____

1
0

2
1
0

5. **(continued)**

(*c*)   A hide mallet and former were used to shape the brass sheet.

State a reason for using a hide mallet in preference to a ball pein hammer.

_____

1
0

(*d*)   The brass sheet *work hardened* when shaped. It was *annealed* to make it *malleable*.

Explain the terms *work hardened*, *annealed* and *malleable*.

1   Work hardened _____

1
0
1
0
1
0

2   Annealed _____

3   Malleable _____

(*e*)   The clock face is made from a thermoplastic.

State what is meant by the term "thermoplastic".

_____

1
0

(*f*)   State **two** benefits of using a thermoplastic for the clock face.

1 _____

1
0
1
0

2 _____

(*g*)   Thirty clocks are to be made.

State **one** method that would speed up production.

_____

1
0

[Turn over

DO NOT
WRITE IN
THIS
MARGIN

6. A child's toy bike is shown below.

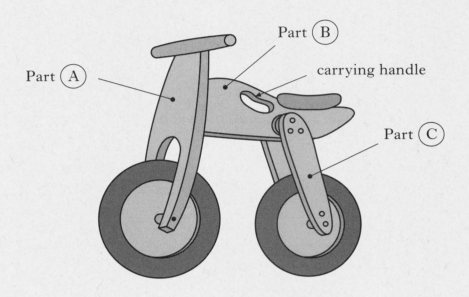

Part (A)   Part (B)   carrying handle   Part (C)

(a) Parts (A), (B) and (C) are made from plywood.

State **two** reasons for this choice of material.

1 _____

2 _____

(b) State the name of a **machine** tool that could be used to cut the shape of Part (A).

_____

(c) An incomplete sequence of operations for the manufacture of the carrying handle is shown.

(i) State the operation carried out at step 2.

Step 1   mark out waste using a template

Step 2   _____

Step 3   remove waste using a coping saw

waste

1
0
1
0

1
0

1
0

6. (c) **(continued)**

(ii) Describe how a coping saw is adjusted when cutting the outline shape of the carrying handle.

_____

_____

_____

2
1
0

(d) Part Ⓒ , the rear forks, were made in pairs.

State **one** method of ensuring that both parts are identical.

_____

1
0

(e) Holes of the type shown below are made in the rear forks.

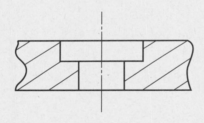

Sectional view of hole

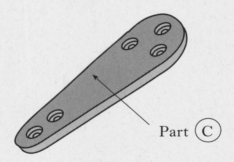

Part Ⓒ

The tools shown below were used to drill the holes in the rear forks.

Tool 1

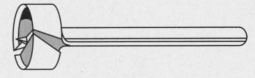

Tool 2

(i) State the full name of each tool.

Tool 1 _____

Tool 2 _____

1
0
1
0

DO NOT
WRITE IN
THIS
MARGIN

6. (e)   (continued)

(ii)   State a reason why tool 2 was used before tool 1 when drilling the holes.

_____

_____

1
0

(f)   Name and sketch a suitable method of joining the handlebar to Part Ⓐ.

Name of jointing method_____

Sketch of jointing method

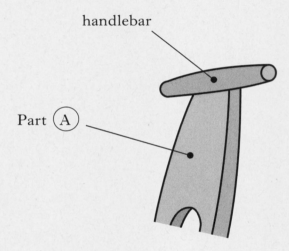

handlebar

Part Ⓐ

1
0

1
0

(g)   The bike was finished in primary colours.

State one reason for using primary colours.

_____

1
0

[*END OF QUESTION PAPER*]

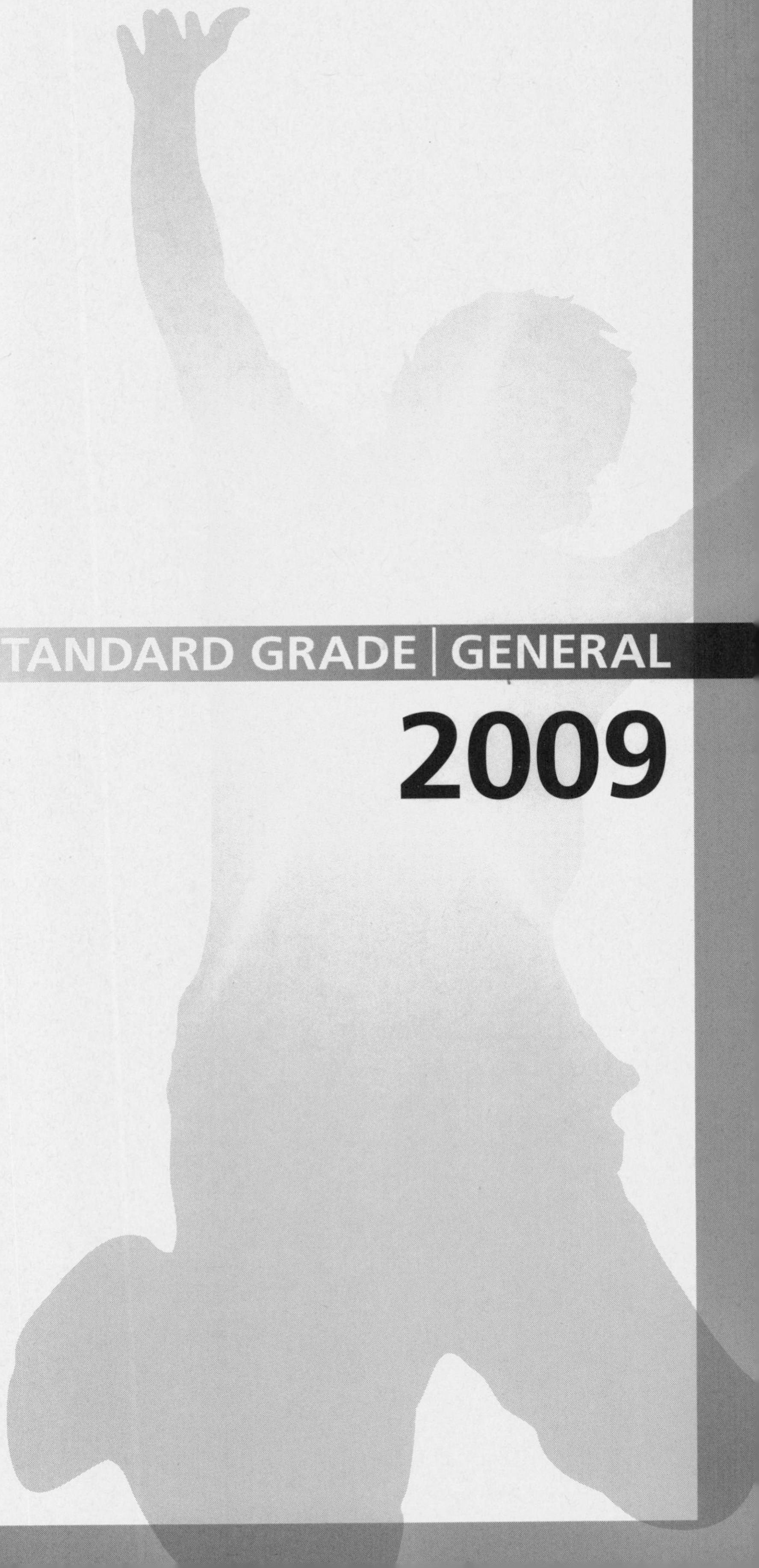

STANDARD GRADE | GENERAL

2009

[BLANK PAGE]

FOR OFFICIAL USE

G

Total

0600/402

NATIONAL
QUALIFICATIONS
2009

MONDAY, 18 MAY
10.20 AM – 11.20 AM

CRAFT AND DESIGN
STANDARD GRADE
General Level

Fill in these boxes and read what is printed below.

Full name of centre

Town

Forename(s)

Surname

Date of birth
Day Month Year   Scottish candidate number   Number of seat

1 Answer all the questions.

2 Read every question carefully before you answer.

3 Write your answers in the spaces provided.

4 Do **not** write in the margins.

5 All dimensions are given in millimetres.

6 Before leaving the examination room you must give this book to the invigilator. If you do not, you may lose all the marks for this paper.

DO NOT WRITE IN THIS MARGIN

ATTEMPT ALL QUESTIONS

1. The wooden clothes hanger shown below is designed to hang in a wardrobe or be freestanding.

Base

(a) The wood joints shown below were considered during the design of the hanger.
State the name of each joint.

X   Y   Z

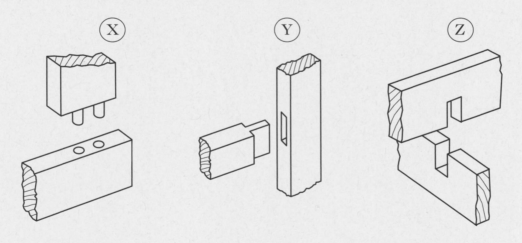

Joint (X) _____

Joint (Y) _____

Joint (Z) _____

1
0
1
0
1
0

1. (continued)

(b) One half of joint (Z) is shown below.

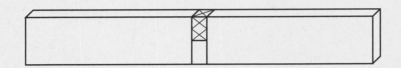

(i) The tools used to mark out the joint are shown below. State the names of these tools.

Tool (A)   Tool (B)

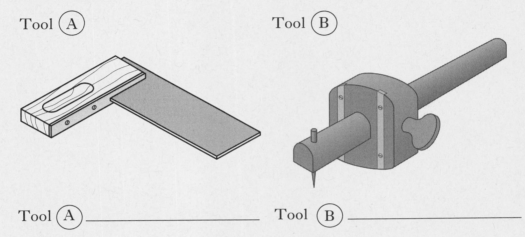

Tool (A) _____   Tool (B) _____

(ii) The tools used in the manufacture of the joint are shown below. State the names of these tools.

Tool (C)   Tool (D)

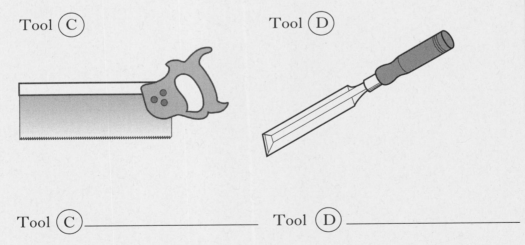

Tool (C) _____   Tool (D) _____

(c) Varnish was applied to the hanger. State **two** reasons for applying a varnish finish.

Reason 1 _____

Reason 2 _____

Page three   **[Turn over**

DO NOT
WRITE IN
THIS
MARGIN

2. A mild steel, wall mounted coat rack is shown.

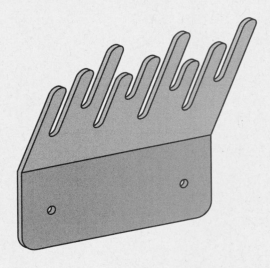

(a) The coat rack was marked out using the following tools. State the name and use of each tool.

(i) Name _____

Use _____

_____

_____

1
0

1
0

(ii) Name _____

Use _____

_____

_____

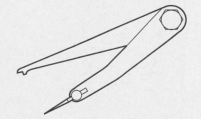

1
0

(iii) Name _____

Use _____

_____

_____

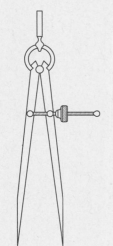

1
0

1
0

1
0

2.   **(continued)**

(*b*)   The following machine was used in the manufacture of the coat rack.

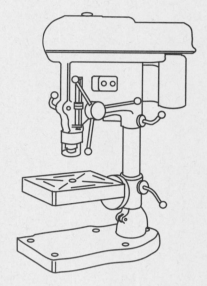

(i)   State the name of this machine. _____

1
0

(ii)   State **two** safety checks that should be carried out before starting the machine.

Check 1 _____

1
0

Check 2 _____

1
0

(*c*)   The following tool was used when forming the coat rack.

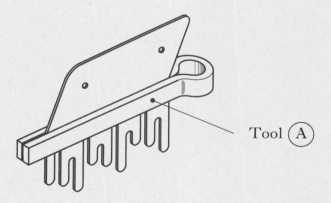

Tool (A)

State the name of tool (A). _____

1
0

(*d*)   State a suitable finish, apart from paint, that could be applied to the coat rack.

_____

1
0

DO NOT
WRITE II
THIS
MARGIN

3.   A design for a DVD storage unit is shown below.

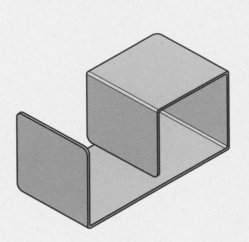 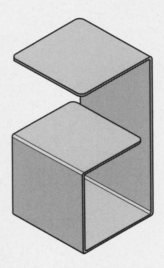

(*a*)   (i)   State **two** factors that would affect the overall size of the unit.

1 _____

2 _____

1
0
1
0

(ii)   Metal and plastic were considered as possible materials for the unit. State the name of a suitable:

Non-ferrous metal; _____

Thermoplastic. _____

1
0
1
0

(*b*)   An incomplete design specification for the unit is given below.   Complete the design specification using each of the given design factors.

Design factor	Specification statement
Material	Must be made from a single piece of thermoplastic
Aesthetics	_____
	_____
Ergonomics	_____
	_____
Safety	_____
	_____

1
0

1
0

1
0

3. **(continued)**

(*c*) (i) Complete the sequence of operations required to finish the edges of the thermoplastic storage unit.

    1.   Cross file the edge flat

    2.   _____

    3.   Use "wet and dry" paper

    4.   _____

  (ii) State why it is easier to finish the edges before the thermoplastic is bent.

    _____

    _____

(*d*) The equipment shown below was used to heat the thermoplastic before bending.

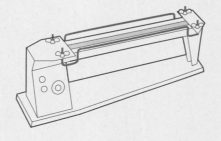

  (i) State the name of this machine. _____

  (ii) State a safety precaution that should be followed when handling hot plastic.

    _____

  (iii) State what would happen if the plastic is not hot enough before it is bent.

    _____

(*e*) State the name of the stage in the design process when the finished DVD unit is tested.

    _____

1
0

1
0

1
0

1
0

1
0

1
0

1
0

DO NOT
WRITE IN
THIS
MARGIN

4.   A holder for remote controls is shown below.

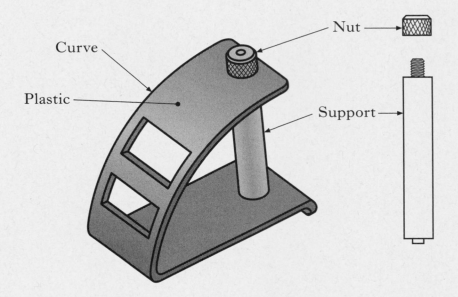

(a)   The remote controls were measured as part of the design process.

State the stage in the design process when this would have been carried out.

_____

(b)   Aluminium and steel bars identical in length and diameter were available for the support. State **two** ways in which the aluminium bar could be identified from the steel bar.

1 _____

2 _____

(c)   State a reason why the plastic supplied for the body had a polythene covering on it.

_____

(d)   State the name of the equipment used to heat the plastic before forming the curve.

_____

4.   (continued)

(e)   The machine below was used to manufacture the support and nut.

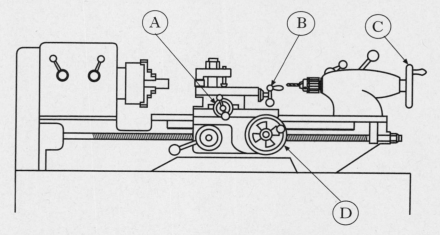

(i)   Name this machine. _____

          1
          0

Handles (A), (B), (C) and (D) are shown on the machine above.

Select the correct handle to use when carrying out the following processes.

(ii)   Parallel turning the support

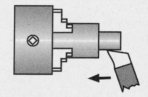

        Handle _____

          1
          0

(iii)   Drilling the nut

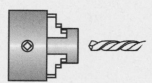

        Handle _____

          1
          0

(f)   The pattern on the nut was created using the tool shown below.

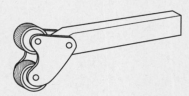

State the name of the process used to create the pattern on the nut.

_____

          1
          0

DO NOT
WRITE IN
THIS
MARGIN

5. A wooden kitchen roll holder is shown below.

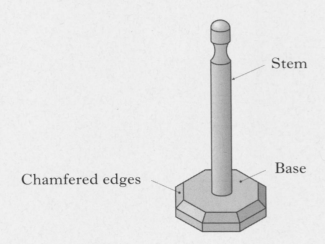

(a) The following statement appeared in the specification. "The holder must be stable."

State which feature of the holder gives it stability.

_____

1
0

(b) The stem is turned on a wood lathe as shown below.

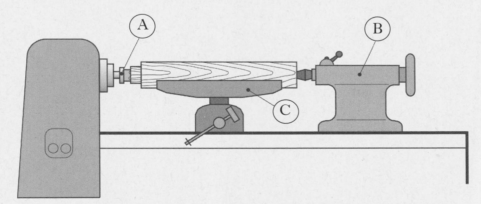

From the list below select the name of parts Ⓐ , Ⓑ and Ⓒ .

Revolving centre   Tailstock   Headstock   Fork centre   Tool rest

(i)   Part Ⓐ _____

1
0

(ii) Part Ⓑ _____

1
0

(iii) Part Ⓒ _____

1
0

DO NOT WRITE IN THIS MARGIN

5. (continued)

(*c*) State **two** safety checks which should be made to the wood lathe before switching it on.

1 ______________________________

______________________________ 1 0

2 ______________________________

______________________________ 1 0

(*d*) The edges of the base were chamfered. State the name of a hand tool used to chamfer the edges.

______________________________ 1 0

(*e*) The wooden base was varnished. State **two** stages in the preparation of the base before applying the varnish.

Stage 1 ______________________________

______________________________ 1 0

Stage 2 ______________________________

______________________________ 1 0

[Turn over

6. A school enterprise group made table mats from contrasting strips of wood as shown below.

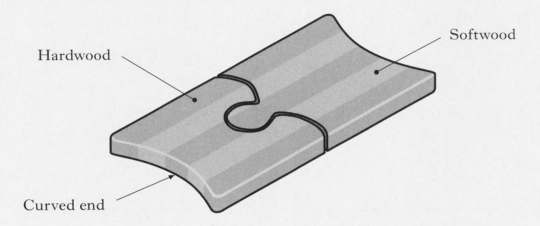

Hardwood

Softwood

Curved end

(a) A list of materials is given below.

Hardboard   Pine   Plywood   Beech   Blockboard

From the list select:

(i) a hardwood; _____

(ii) a softwood. _____

1
0

1
0

(b) One stage in the manufacture of the mat is shown.

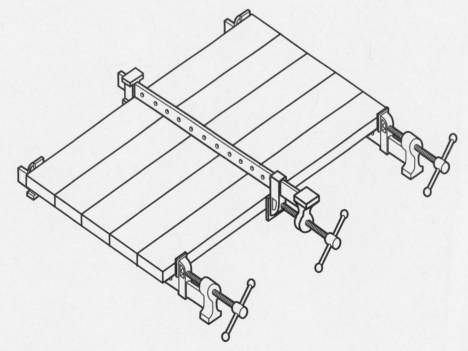

(i) State the name of a suitable wood glue.

_____

1
0

6. **(b)** **(continued)**

(ii) The holding device shown below was used to hold the strips while the glue dried.

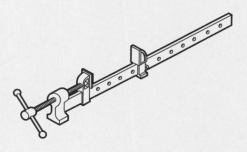

State the name of this device. _____

1
0

(c) A number of mats were produced for sale.

State **two** advantages of using a template to mark out the curved ends.

1 _____

_____

1
0

2 _____

_____

1
0

(d) State the name of a **machine** tool and a **hand** tool suitable for cutting out the curved ends.

(i) Machine tool _____

1
0

(ii) Hand tool _____

1
0

[END OF QUESTION PAPER]

[BLANK PAGE]

STANDARD GRADE | CREDIT

2009

[BLANK PAGE]

FOR OFFICIAL USE

C

Total
Mark

0600/403

NATIONAL
QUALIFICATIONS
2009

MONDAY, 18 MAY
1.00 PM – 2.00 PM

CRAFT AND DESIGN
STANDARD GRADE
Credit Level

Fill in these boxes and read what is printed below.

Full name of centre

Town

Forename(s)

Surname

Date of birth
Day Month Year   Scottish candidate number   Number of seat

1 Answer all the questions.

2 Read every question carefully before you answer.

3 Write your answers in the spaces provided.

4 Do **not** write in the margins.

5 All dimensions are given in millimetres.

6 Before leaving the examination room you must give this book to the invigilator. If you do not, you may lose all the marks for this paper.

PB 0600/403 6/12020

DO NOT
WRITE IN
THIS
MARGIN

ATTEMPT ALL QUESTIONS

1. A magazine rack manufactured from acrylic is shown below.

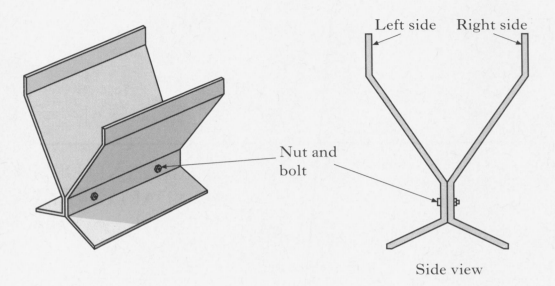

Left side   Right side

Nut and bolt

Side view

(a) Acrylic is a thermoplastic.

State what is meant by the term thermoplastic.

_____

1
0

(b) State **two** reasons why acrylic was considered a suitable material for the manufacture of the magazine rack.

(i) _____

1
0

(ii) _____

1
0

(c) State **one** disadvantage of using acrylic.

1
0

_____

DO NOT
WRITE IN
THIS
MARGIN

1. (continued)

Shown below are the acrylic sheets prior to bending.

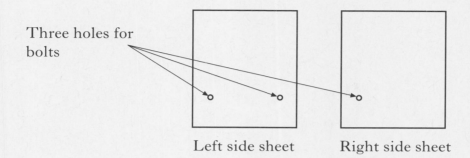

Three holes for bolts

Left side sheet   Right side sheet

(*d*)   State why only three holes were drilled at this stage.

_____

_____

1
0

(*e*)   A number of the magazine racks are to be made.

State how the magazine racks could be bent to an identical shape.

_____

1
0

[Turn over

DO NOT
WRITE IN
THIS
MARGIN

2.   A stainless steel park bench is shown below.

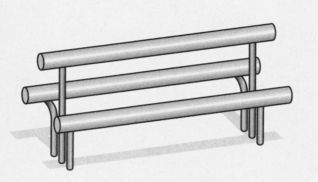 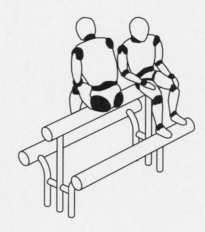

(a)   The primary function of the bench is seating.

State a secondary function of this park bench.

_____

1
0

(b)   The designer used a table of human dimensions when designing the park bench.

(i)   State the name of this type of data.

_____

1
0

(ii)   State the stage in the design process when this data would be gathered.

_____

1
0

(iii)   The bench was designed to suit a range of people between the 5th and 95th percentiles.

State a reason why people below the 5th percentile would find the bench difficult to use.

_____

1
0

(c)   Stainless steel, a ferrous metal, was used in the manufacture of the bench.

(i)   State what is meant by the term ferrous metal.

_____

1
0

(ii)   State **two** reasons why stainless steel is a suitable material for the park bench.

1 _____

1
0

2 _____

1
0

DO NOT
WRITE IN
THIS
MARGIN

2. (continued)

(*d*) The bolt shown below is used to assemble the bench.

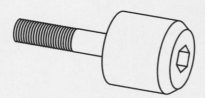

Some of the processes used to manufacture the bolt on a metal work lathe are shown below.

Process (A)   Process (B)

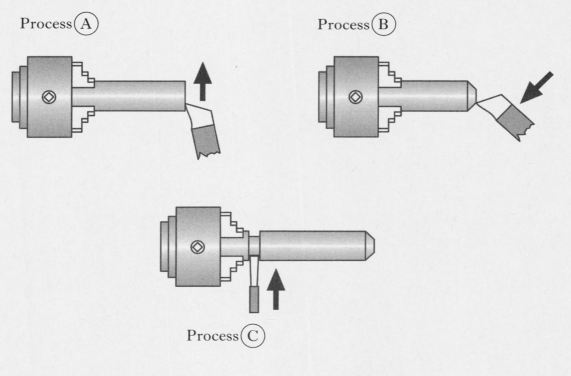

Process (C)

(i)   State the name of process (A).

_____

(ii) State a reason for the 45 degree chamfer at process (B).

_____

(iii) State the name of the slide that would need to be adjusted when turning the chamfer at process (B).

_____

(iv) State the name of process (C).

_____

1
0

1
0

1
0

1
0

DO NOT
WRITE IN
THIS
MARGIN

2. **(continued)**

(*e*)   State **two** procedures or adjustments that ensure a high quality finish is achieved when turning metal.

1 _____

2 _____

(*f*)   The tool shown below was used during the manufacture of the bolt.

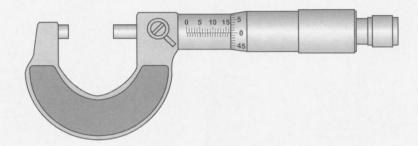

   (i)   State the name of this tool.

   _____

   (ii)   State a reason why this tool was used rather than a pair of outside callipers.

   _____

(*g*)   The tool shown below was used to cut the thread on the bolt.

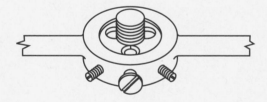

State **two** procedures that ensure a high quality thread is cut on the bolt.

1 _____

2 _____

1
0
1
0

1
0

1
0

1
0
1
0

3. Hexagonal wall shelves are shown below.

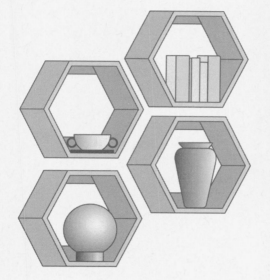

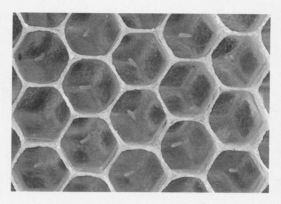

Honeycomb

A thematic approach helped inspire the design for the shelves.

(a) State one other technique that can be used to generate ideas.

_____

1
0

(b) Aesthetics were considered when designing the shelves.
     State what is meant by the term aesthetics.

_____

1
0

(c) Proportion is considered an important aesthetic factor.
     State **three** other aesthetic factors.

  (i) _____

1
0

  (ii) _____

1
0

  (iii) _____

1
0

(d) The shelves are made of plywood.
     Describe the constructional feature that gives plywood its strength.
     Sketches may be used to illustrate your answer.

_____

_____

_____

_____

1
0

DO NOT
WRITE I[]
THIS
MARGI[]

4. A school enterprise group designed and made the vase shown below.

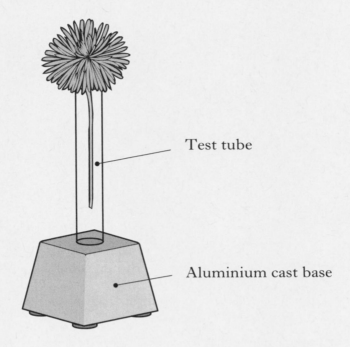

Test tube

Aluminium cast base

(a)   Market research was carried out during the investigation stage of the design process.

   (i)   Explain the purpose of market research.

   _____

   (ii)   Describe how market research could be carried out.

   _____

(b)   During the design process models were produced.

   State **two** reasons why modelling is used in the design process.

   (i) _____

   (ii) _____

1
0

1
0

1
0
1
0

4. (continued)

(c)   Sand casting was used during the manufacture of the base.

In order to cast the aluminium base, a wooden pattern was produced.

Wooden pattern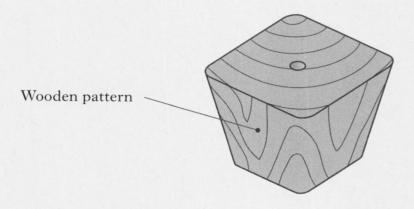

State **two** features of the pattern that would allow it to be easily removed from the moulding sand.

(i) _____

(ii) _____

1
0
1
0

(d)   Other than aesthetic reasons, state why the school enterprise group used aluminium for casting.

_____

1
0

(e)   The cast body is shown below.

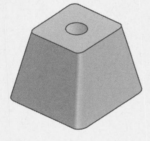

Blind hole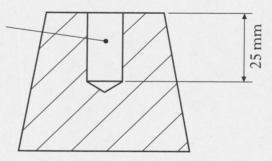

25 mm

View of cast body

Sectional view of cast body

A blind hole was drilled using a pedestal drill.

State a method of ensuring the depth is 25 mm.

_____

_____

1
0

DO NOT
WRITE IN
THIS
MARGIN

5. A candle holder is shown below.

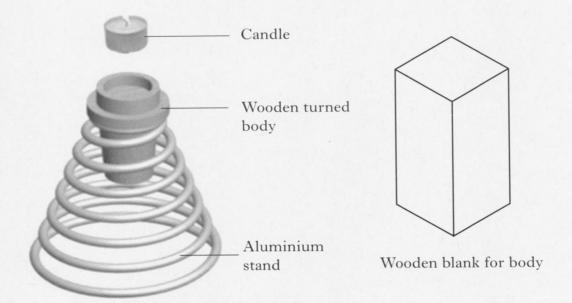

Candle

Wooden turned
body

Aluminium
stand

Wooden blank for body

(*a*) The wooden body was manufactured from a blank on a wood lathe.

Describe three stages in preparing a wooden blank before fitting to the lathe.
Sketches may be used to illustrate your answer.

Stage 1

_____

_____

_____

_____

Stage 2

_____

_____

_____

_____

1
0

1
0

DO NOT
WRITE IN
THIS
MARGIN

5. (a) (continued)

Stage 3

_____

_____

_____

_____

1
0

(b)   The wooden body is shown below.

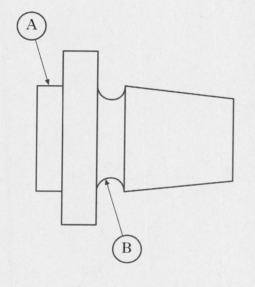 

(i)   State the name of the turning tool used to produce the square shoulder shown at Ⓐ.

_____

1
0

(ii)   State the name of the turning tool used to produce the groove shown at Ⓑ.

_____

1
0

(iii)   When wood turning, state an advantage of using a revolving (live) centre rather than a dead centre.

_____

1
0

[Turn over

DO NOT
WRITE I
THIS
MARGIN

5. **(continued)**

(c)   The tool below was used in the manufacture of the candle holder.

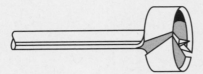

State the name of this tool.

_____

1
0

(d)   During the manufacture of the stand it was necessary to anneal the aluminium.

(i)   State the purpose of annealing aluminium.

_____

1
0

(ii)   Describe the process of annealing aluminium.

_____

_____

_____

2
1
0

6. A folding deck chair is shown below.

Nylon seat
and back
support

Hardwood frame

Chair folded

(a)   State **two** advantages that a folding chair has over a non-folding chair.

Advantage 1

_____

Advantage 2

_____

(b)   Ergonomics was considered when designing the chair.

(i)   State what is meant by ergonomics.

_____

(ii)   State an ergonomic reason for using nylon material for the seat and back support.

_____

(c)   The frame of the chair is made of hardwood.

State the name of a suitable hardwood.

_____

[Turn over

1
0

1
0

1
0

1
0

1
0

DO NOT
WRITE IN
THIS
MARGIN

7. A decorative wooden box and stand are shown below.

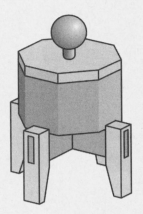

Assembled box

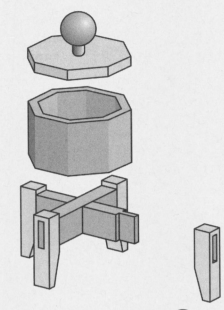

Exploded view showing joint Ⓐ

(*a*)   State the name of joint Ⓐ .

_____

1
0

The tool shown below was used to mark out the joint.

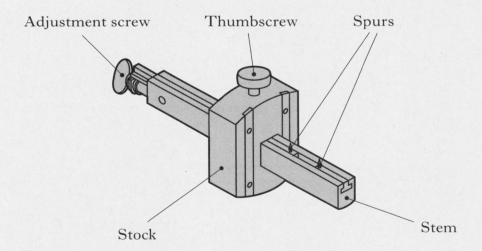

Adjustment screw   Thumbscrew   Spurs

Stock   Stem

(*b*)   (i)   State the name of this tool.

_____

1
0

(ii) State two adjustments that can be made to this tool.

Adjustment 1 _____

Adjustment 2 _____

1
0
1
0

7. (continued)

(c)   State the name of another joint that could have been used as an alternative to joint (A).

_____

1
0

(d)   Joint (A) was "dry clamped".

State the purpose of dry clamping.

_____

_____

_____

1
0

(e)   The tool below was used in the manufacture of the box.

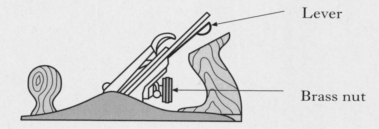

Lever

Brass nut

(i)   State the purpose of the lever.

_____

1
0

(ii)   State the purpose of the brass nut.

_____

1
0

[END OF QUESTION PAPER]

[BLANK PAGE]

STANDARD GRADE | GENERAL

2010

[BLANK PAGE]

G

FOR OFFICIAL USE

Q1		Q5	
Q2		Q6	
Q3		Q7	
Q4			

Total

0600/402

NATIONAL QUALIFICATIONS 2010

MONDAY, 17 MAY 10.20 AM – 11.20 AM

CRAFT AND DESIGN STANDARD GRADE
General Level

Fill in these boxes and read what is printed below.

Full name of centre

Town

Forename(s)

Surname

Date of birth

Day   Month   Year

Scottish candidate number

Number of seat

1 Answer all the questions.

2 Read every question carefully before you answer.

3 Write your answers in the spaces provided.

4 Do **not** write in the margins.

5 All dimensions are given in millimetres.

6 Before leaving the examination room you must give this book to the Invigilator. If you do not, you may lose all the marks for this paper.

PB 0600/402 6/18910

DO NOT
WRITE IN
THIS
MARGIN

ATTEMPT ALL QUESTIONS

1. A rocking horse is shown below.

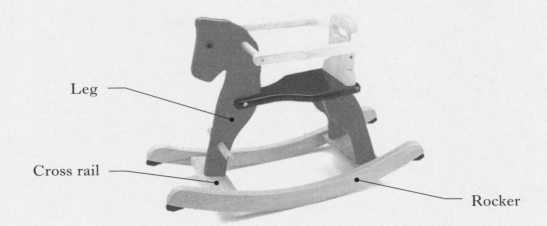

Leg

Cross rail

Rocker

(a) The rocking horse is made from a softwood.

State the name of a suitable softwood.

_____

1
0

(b) Two joints used in the manufacture of the rocking horse are shown below.
State the name of each joint.

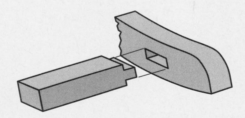

Name _____

1
0

Name _____

1
0

1. (continued)

(*c*) A butt joint was considered for joining the leg to the cross rail as shown.

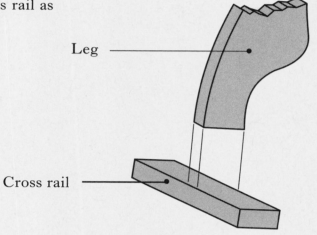

Leg

Cross rail

State **one** reason why this joint was rejected.

_____

1
0

(*d*) The following tools were used in the manufacture of the rocking horse. State the name of each tool.

(i)

Tool _____

1
0

(ii)

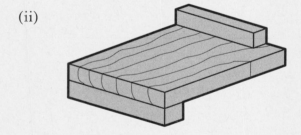

Tool _____

1
0

(iii)

Tool _____

1
0

DO NOT
WRITE IN
THIS
MARGIN

2. A table lamp is shown below.

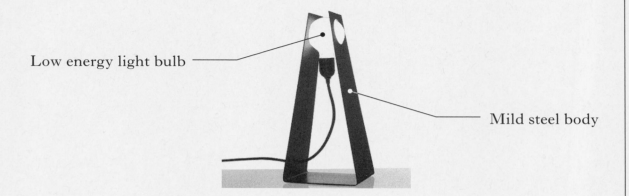

Low energy light bulb

Mild steel body

(*a*) One statement in the specification for the table lamp is given below.

- The body of the lamp must be made from mild steel.

List two other statements that could appear in the design specification.

(i) _____

(ii) _____

(*b*) The body is made from mild steel.

State a reason for this choice of material.

_____

(*c*) The sketch below shows the body marked out on the mild steel.

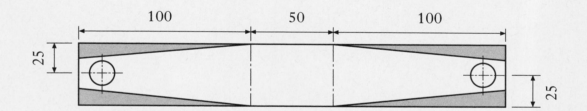

State the minimum amount of material required to manufacture the body.

Length of material _____

Width of material _____

2. **(continued)**

(*d*)   (i)   A scriber rather than a pencil was used to mark out the lamp on the mild steel.

State a reason for using a scriber rather than a pencil.

_____

1
0

The tools shown below were used during the manufacture of the lamp.
State the name and purpose of each tool.

(ii)   Name _____

1
0

(iii)   Purpose _____

_____

1
0

(iv)   Name _____

1
0

(v)   Purpose _____

_____

1
0

(*e*)   A finish was applied to the mild steel body.

(i)   State **two** reasons for applying a finish to the mild steel body.

1 _____

1
0

2 _____

1
0

(ii)   After manufacture the lamp was tested and it was found to scratch the surface it was sitting on.

State the stage in the design process when this fault showed up.

_____

1
0

[Turn over

3. A pencil holder is shown below.

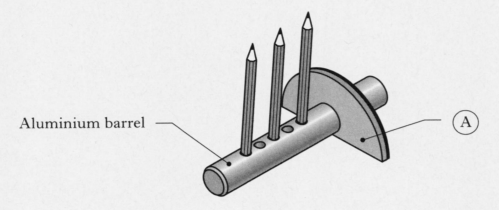

Aluminium barrel

(A)

(*a*) State the function of part (A).

_____

1
0

(*b*) Aluminium was selected for the barrel of the pencil holder.

State a reason why aluminium makes a suitable choice of material for the barrel.

_____

1
0

(*c*) The aluminium barrel was cut into two parts using a hand tool.

State the name of a suitable tool.

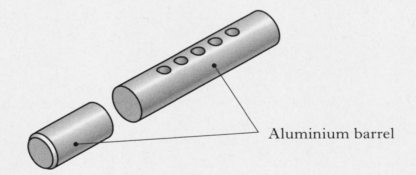

Aluminium barrel

_____

1
0

3. **(continued)**

(d) The barrel was manufactured on the metal lathe, shown below.

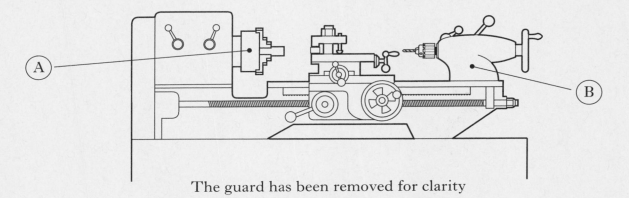

The guard has been removed for clarity

(i) State the name of part (A).

_____

**1
0**

(ii) State the name of part (B).

_____

**1
0**

(e) State **two** safety checks that should be observed when using a metal lathe.

1 _____

**1
0**

2 _____

**1
0**

(f) Three steps in the manufacture of the barrel are shown.

Name the turning process at (X) and (Y) and the drill used in (Z).

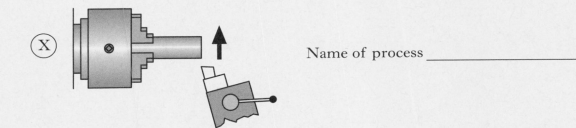

Name of process _____

**1
0**

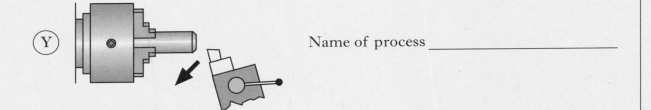

Name of process _____

**1
0**

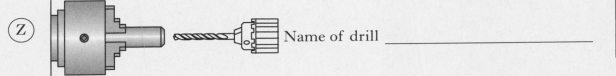

Name of drill _____

**1
0**

4. A kitchen roll holder is shown below.

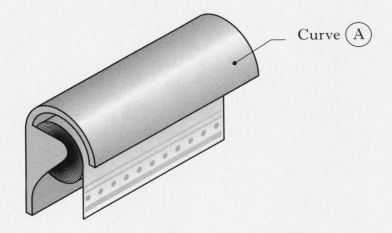

Curve Ⓐ

(*a*) During the design process, the following design factors were considered.

Materials   Safety   Aesthetics   Function   Environment

Complete the diagram below by using the **word bank** above.

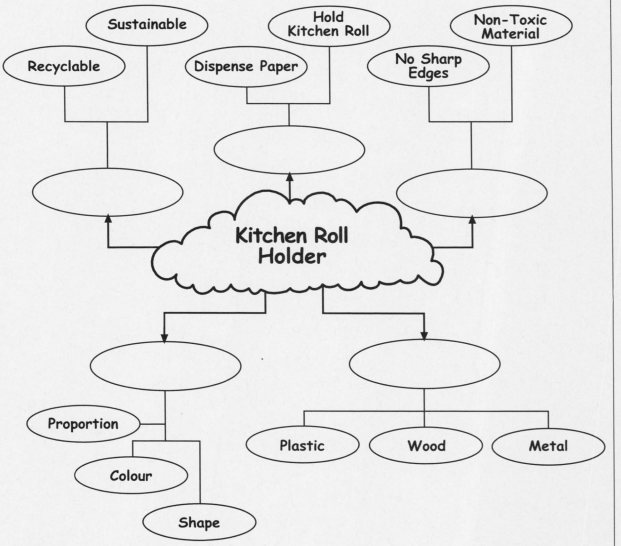

4. **(continued)**

(*b*) The kitchen roll holder was made from a thermoplastic.

State the name of a suitable thermoplastic.

_____

The plastic is marked out as shown below.

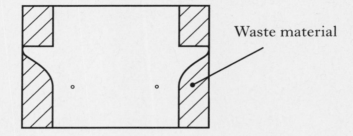

Waste material

(*c*) (i) Select from the list below the name of the equipment used to hold the plastic, while cutting the outline of the holder.

Bench vice   G-clamp   Hand vice   Sash cramp

Name of equipment

_____

(ii) The holder was cut out using the saw shown below.

State the name of this saw.

_____

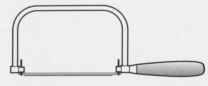

(iii) Complete the stages for finishing the edges of the plastic.

1   cross file down to the marked line

2   _____

3   use wet and dry paper

4   _____

(iv) The plastic was heated before the curve at (A) was produced.

State the name of the piece of equipment used to heat the plastic.

_____

1
0

1
0

1
0

1
0

1
0

1
0

[**Turn over**

DO NOT
WRITE IN
THIS
MARGIN

5. A trophy is shown.

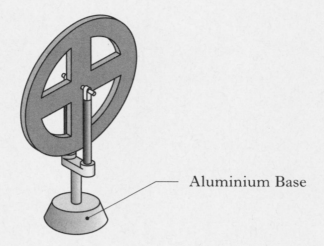

Aluminium Base

(a) During the manufacture of the base, molten aluminium was poured into a sand mould. Select the name of this process from the list below.

Forging   Casting   Welding   Turning

Name of process

_____

1
0

(b) State a property of aluminium that makes it a suitable material for using this process in schools.

_____

1
0

(c) A cross section of the moulding boxes are shown below.

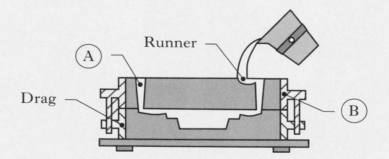

(i) State the name of the opening at (A).

_____

1
0

(ii) State the name of box (B).

_____

1
0

(iii) State the name of one piece of protective clothing, apart from gloves and facemask that should be worn when pouring molten aluminium.

_____

1
0

6. The thermoplastic dish shown below was made for a school food and drinks challenge.

Dish

(a) The thermoplastic was heated and formed to produce the dish shown.

State the name of the process used to produce the dish.

_____

1
0

(b) The wooden pattern shown below was used during the manufacture of the dish.

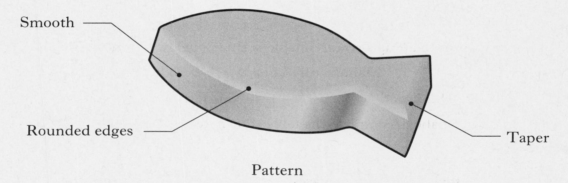

Smooth

Rounded edges

Taper

Pattern

State which feature on the pattern would:

(i) prevent the plastic from tearing;

_____

1
0

(ii) help with the removal of the dish from the pattern.

_____

1
0

[Turn over

DO NOT
WRITE IN
THIS
MARGIN

7. A toothbrush holder is shown below.

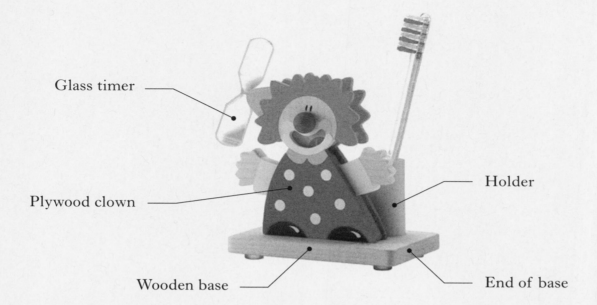

Glass timer

Plywood clown

Wooden base

Holder

End of base

(a) A timer is shown in the design of the toothbrush holder.

State a reason for the timer.

1
0

(b) An incomplete materials research table is shown below.

Ferrous   Manufactured board   Thermoplastic
Hardwood   Non-ferrous

Using the list above complete the table shown below.

Material	Classification	Description
Mild steel		Magnetic, tough
Plywood		Multi-layered board
Mahogany		Close grained, reddish brown in colour
Acrylic		Available in many colours can be heated and shaped
Aluminium		Lightweight, silver coloured

1
0

1
0

1
0

1
0

1
0

1
0

7. (continued)

(c) During the design process a working drawing was produced.

State **one** piece of information you would find from a working drawing.

_____

10

(d) A machine was used to smooth the ends of the wooden base.

State the name of a suitable machine.

_____

10

(e) State the name of a **hand tool** and a **machine tool** that could be used to cut out the plywood clown.

(i) Hand tool _____

10

(ii) Machine tool _____

10

(f) The client stated that the toothbrush holder was to be finished in primary colours.

State a reason for using primary colours.

_____

10

[END OF QUESTION PAPER]

[BLANK PAGE]

[BLANK PAGE]

FOR OFFICIAL USE

C

Q1		Q5	
Q2		Q6	
Q3		Q7	
Q4			

Total Mark

0600/403

NATIONAL QUALIFICATIONS 2010

MONDAY, 17 MAY 1.00 PM – 2.00 PM

CRAFT & DESIGN
STANDARD GRADE
Credit Level

Fill in these boxes and read what is printed below.

Full name of centre

Town

Forename

Surname

Date of birth

Day   Month   Year   Scottish candidate number   Number of seat

1. Answer all the questions.

2. Read every question carefully before you answer.

3. Write your answers in the spaces provided.

4. Do **not** write in the margins.

5. All dimensions are given in millimetres.

6. Before leaving the examination room you must give this book to the Invigilator. If you do not, you may lose all the marks for this paper.

DO NOT
WRITE IN
THIS
MARGIN

ATTEMPT ALL QUESTIONS

1. A table is shown below.

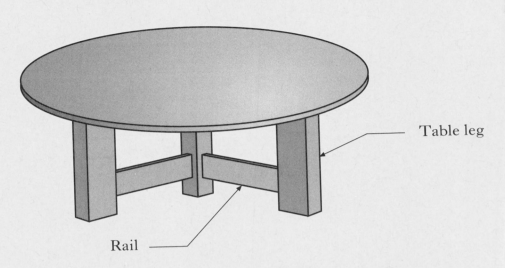

Table leg

Rail

(a) The tool shown below was used in the manufacture of the table legs.

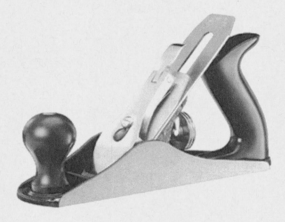

State two separate adjustments that can be made to this tool.

Adjustment one

_____

_____

1
0

Adjustment two

_____

_____

1
0

1. (continued)

(b) The mortise gauge shown below was used to mark out the mortise and tenon joints.

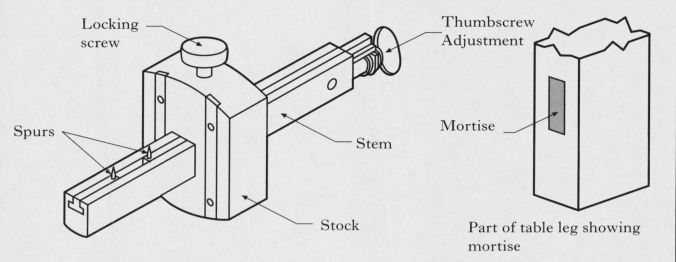

Locking screw

Thumbscrew Adjustment

Spurs

Stem

Mortise

Stock

Part of table leg showing mortise

Describe two steps to mark a 12 mm mortise centrally on the table leg.

Sketches may be used to illustrate your answer.

Step 1

_____

_____

_____

_____

_____

Step 2

_____

_____

_____

_____

_____

1
0

1
0

(c) The finishing process includes "wetting the wood".

State the purpose of "wetting the wood".

_____

1
0

DO NOT
WRITE IN
THIS
MARGIN

2. A woodpecker toy is shown below.

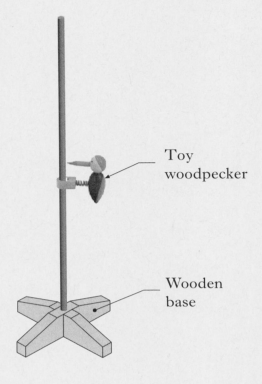

Toy
woodpecker

Wooden
base

Enlarged view of toy woodpecker

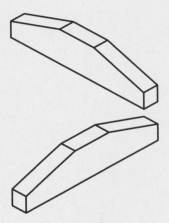

View of parts for base

(a) During the design process various techniques were used to generate ideas.

Name two techniques used by designers to help generate ideas.

(i) _____

(ii) _____

(b) The woodpecker is made from a close grained hardwood.

State the name of a suitable hardwood.

_____

(c) The wooden base is made in two parts.

State the name of a suitable joint for the base of the toy.

_____

1
0
1
0

1
0

1
0

2. (continued)

The woodpecker's body was turned on a woodwork lathe.

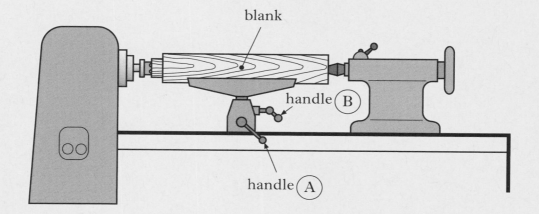

(d) The tool rest can be adjusted before the wood lathe is switched on.

State three adjustments that can be made to the tool rest.

(i) _____

(ii) _____

(iii) _____

(e) The blank was turned to a cylinder

State the name of a turning tool used to produce the cylinder.

_____

(f) A tool was used to check the diameter of the cylinder.

State the name of a suitable tool.

_____

(g) State an adjustment that could be made to the woodwork lathe to improve the finish of the woodpecker.

_____

[Turn over

DO NOT
WRITE IN
THIS
MARGIN

3. A model spaceship on a stand is shown below.

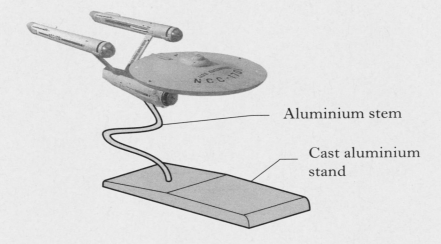

Aluminium stem

Cast aluminium
stand

(a) The stand was manufactured by sand casting.

Small holes above pattern

Pattern

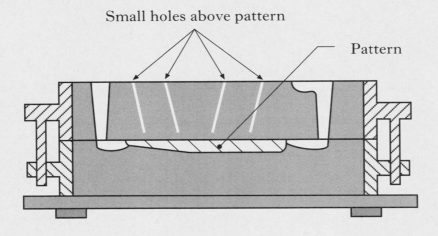

(i) The pattern for the stand has tapered sides.

State a reason for this feature.

_____

1
0

(ii) Parting powder was used during the manufacture of the stand.

State the purpose of parting powder.

_____

1
0

(b) Small holes are made in the sand above the pattern. State a reason for these holes.

_____

1
0

3. (continued)

(c) One end of the stem is threaded.

   (i) State how the end of the stem should be prepared before threading.

_____

_____

1 0

The tool shown below was used to cut the thread on the stem.

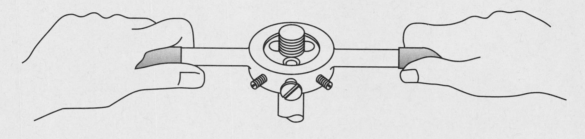

   (ii) State the name of this tool.

_____

1 0

   (iii) The initial thread was cut and found to be a tight fit.

Describe how to adjust the tool so that the thread is an "easy running fit".

_____

_____

_____

2 1 0

(d) The aluminium stem was heat treated to make it more malleable.

   (i) State what is meant by malleable.

_____

1 0

   (ii) State the name of the heat treatment process.

_____

1 0

   (iii) State a reason why soap was used in this process.

_____

_____

1 0

DO NOT
WRITE IN
THIS
MARGIN

4. A can crusher is shown below.

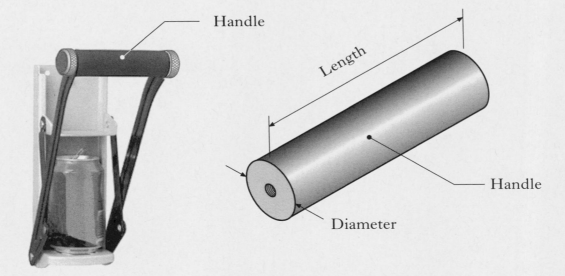

(*a*) During the design of the can crusher, reference was made to data sheets of human dimensions.

State the name of this type of data.

_____

1
0

(*b*) The handle of the crusher has been designed to be used by adults in the 5th to 95th percentile range.

State the percentile used to determine the length of the handle.

_____

1
0

(*c*) An exploded view of the handle is shown below.

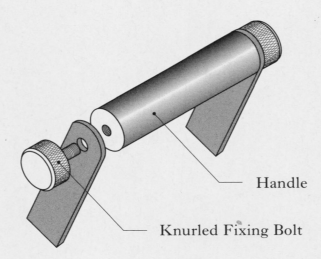

Handle

Knurled Fixing Bolt

4. **(c)** **(continued)**

The handle was manufactured using a metal lathe.

When facing off the handle, a pip remained on the end as shown below.

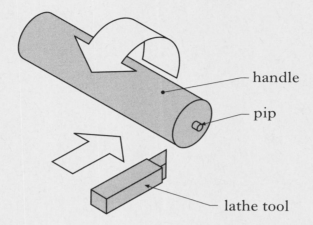

handle

pip

lathe tool

State one fault that would cause this pip.

_____

1
0

(d) The lathe tool shown below was used in the manufacture of the handle.

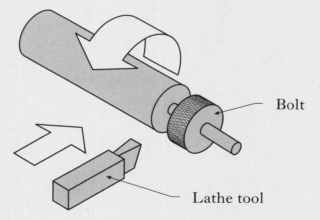

Bolt

Lathe tool

State the name of this lathe tool.

_____

1
0

(e) The bolt was knurled.

  (i) State a reason for knurling the bolt.

_____

1
0

  (ii) State an adjustment to the lathe that may be necessary before knurling.

_____

1
0

DO NOT
WRITE IN
THIS
MARGIN

4. (continued)

(*f*) One end of the handle is shown below.

25 mm

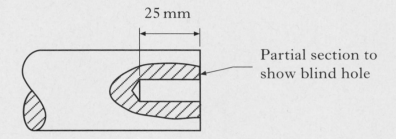

Partial section to
show blind hole

The drill shown below was used in the manufacture of the handle.

(i) State the name of this drill.

_____

(ii) State the function of this drill.

_____

The blind hole was drilled to a depth of 25 mm using the metal lathe.

(iii) Describe a method of ensuring that the hole is drilled to the correct depth.

_____

(*g*) The blind hole was threaded.

(i) State why care must be taken when threading a blind hole.

_____

(ii) State the name of the tap that should be used to begin threading.

_____

(iii) State the name of the tap that should be used to complete the threading.

_____

DO NOT WRITE IN THIS MARGIN

4. (continued)

(*h*) The handle was plastic dip coated.

Describe in detail three stages in the plastic dip coating process.

The stages should be described in order.

Stage 1

1 0

Stage 2

1 0

Stage 3

1 0

(*i*) State a reason why the plastic looked dull and gritty after the dip coating process.

1 0

[Turn over

DO NOT
WRITE IN
THIS
MARGIN

5. A charging stand for a mobile phone is shown below.

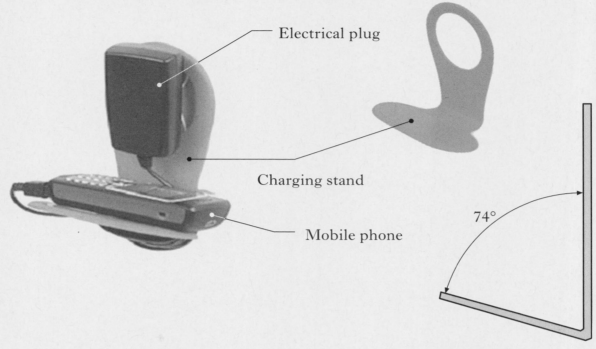

Electrical plug

Charging stand

Mobile phone

74°

Side view of charging stand
showing angle

(a) Aesthetics and ergonomics are design factors.   State three further design factors that may have been considered in the design of the charging stand.

1 _____

2 _____

3 _____

(b) During the design process various types of graphics are used.

  (i) State the name of the stage where rough sketches are used.

    Stage _____

  (ii) State the name of the stage where fully rendered 3D sketches are used.

    Stage _____

(c) A number of identical charging stands are to be manufactured. State two ways in which manufacture can be speeded up.

1 _____

2 _____

6. A pen is shown below.

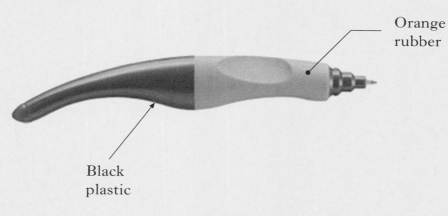

Orange
rubber

Black
plastic

(a) During the design of the pen, ergonomics was considered.

   (i) State what is meant by the term ergonomics.

   _____

   (ii) State two ergonomic features of the pen shown above.

   1 _____

   2 _____

(b) (i) Orange and black are used to contrast with each other.

   State why a designer would use colour contrast on a product.

   _____

   _____

   (ii) State two other methods a designer can use to create contrast in a product.

   1 _____

   _____

   2 _____

   _____

(c) Potential customers were asked to evaluate the pen by means of a questionnaire.

   State the name of this type of research.

   _____

1
0

1
0
1
0

1
0

1
0

1
0

1
0

[Turn over for Question 7 on *Page fourteen*

7. A wall mounted shelf unit made from MDF is shown below.

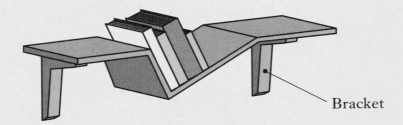

Bracket

(*a*) State two reasons why MDF is a suitable material for the shelves.

1 _____

2 _____

The brackets are fixed to the shelf using countersink screws.

(*b*) On the diagram below, sketch and label the following.

Pilot hole   Countersink hole   Clearance hole

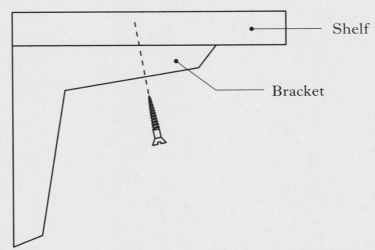

Shelf

Bracket

Side view of bracket and shelf   Use the diagram above to illustrate
                                         your answer

1
0
1
0

1
0
1
0
1
0

[END OF QUESTION PAPER]

[BLANK PAGE]

[BLANK PAGE]